COURAGEOUS SPIRITS

Aboriginal Heroes of Our Children

Teacher's Guide

Jo-ann Archibald

Val Friesen

Canadian Cataloguing in Publication Data

ISBN 0-919441-51-3

1. Indians of North America---Canada---Biography
---Study and teaching. 2. Heroes--Canada--
Biography--Study and teaching. 3. Indians
of North America--Canada--Literary collections.
Study and teaching. I. Archibald, Jo-ann, 1950-
II. Friesen, Val, 1936-   III. Smith, Jeff,
1950-   IV. Sterling, Shirley, 1948-
E78.C2C68 1993 Suppl. 971'.00497 C93-091737-5

The publisher acknowledges the support of the Canada Council, the Cultural
Services Branch of the Province of British Columbia and Department of Indian
and Northern Affairs in the publication of this book.

Production and Design: Jeff Smith, Banjo Terbasket
Cover Design: Banjo Terbasket, Greg Young-Ing, and
                          Jo-ann Archibald

Published by:

Theytus Books Ltd.
P.O. Box 20040
Penticton, B.C. Canada
V2A 8K3

TABLE OF CONTENTS

ACKNOWLEDGMENTS

The writers of this guide wish to acknowledge the generous assistance they have had from individuals and agencies who have contributed human or financial resources to this project.

The Communications Branch of Indian and Northern Affairs Canada and Canada 125 have funded the Aboriginal Heroes Contest, and the book derived from it, *Courageous Spirits: Aboriginal Heroes of Our Children*. This *Teacher's Guide* is also a product of that funding.

We raise our hands in thanks and respect to:

- the Board of Directors, Mokakit Education Research Association for agreeing to host the project, and for their moral support throughout the project development

- the First Nations House of Learning of the University of British Columbia for accommodating the project

- the many participants who contributed to the writing, editing and other development of *Courageous Spirits: Aboriginal Heroes of Our Children*. They have been recognized in the Acknowledgments section of that book

- all the young writers for their thoughtful contributions

- Peg Klesner for the section Beyond *Courageous Spirits...* in this Guide

- Jeff Smith, who with the two of us, wore many hats in developing and editing *Courageous Spirits: Aboriginal Heroes of Our Children*

- Kathy Morven, Project Assistant, for helping in so many ways.

Jo-ann Archibald
Val Friesen

INTRODUCTION

Aboriginal heroes are everywhere...Who is yours? With these words, the Aboriginal Heroes Contest on which this book is based was introduced to students and teachers across Canada.

The heroes theme is an important one. The very concept of *heroes* invokes special images for nearly everyone—of someone who exemplifies courage, moral strength, or other sterling qualities which somehow allow them to exceed the normal bounds that seem to limit human endeavour. (NOTE: for purposes of this book project, the word *hero* is used as a gender-neutral term.)

Children, especially, need heroes as models for their personal striving for excellence. All of us—not just children—need to believe not only that good and honour and courage and freedom exist, but also that these gifts lie within each of us. We also have to know that we can find ways to access them. In short, we need to believe that a hero lies within.

Finding external heroes leads individuals towards discovering the hero within them. The story format offered here is a powerful mechanism for this kind of self-discovery, and, in turn, to the building of self-esteem. **The link between heroes and self-esteem could be the most meaningful approach to using this book with children.**

This Guide has been written to facilitate the use of *Courageous Spirits* with children to show how the book can be used in many ways to provide a rich learning experience for them.

We have provided some ideas for a pedagogical approach consistent with broad teaching principles embedded in values held in common in many Aboriginal cultures. Rather than an authoritative document on the subject, this is a Guide. Rather than offering individual lessons on each piece of student writing, we have provided strategies and practical applications which teachers and parents and others can adapt to their own situations.

Aided by this Guide and the *Courageous Spirits* book, it is our hope that teachers and parents can communicate to students that everyone has something of the heroic in her or him; that everyone can think deeply and feel deeply about issues of importance; and that the path leading to deepest learning involves the mind, body, spirit and emotions.

ORIGINS OF *COURAGEOUS SPIRITS*

Early in 1991, Indian and Northern Affairs Canada developed the concept of a project to promote First Nations role models. Originally entitled *Unsung Native Heroes*, a writing competition lay at the heart of the plan to assemble a collection of "heroes" as identified by Indian and Inuit children. This idea formed the basis of a contract with Mokakit Education Research Association who developed the subsequent writing contest.

The rationale for the project included the following statements:

The objectives of the Aboriginal Heroes contest...can serve here to provide focus for this project. Those are:
- *to promote communication and learning between the youth and Aboriginal community members;*
- *to honour and respect our cultural ways;*
- *to share information about Aboriginal people who have inspired our young people;*
- *to create awareness of Aboriginal cultures and achievements among all school age youth.*

We want to celebrate the fact that as Aboriginal people we have survived generations of assault to our self-esteem and to our cultural ways. Who helped us survive, and how? What values lay at the heart of their actions, and what is their lesson to the world? How might all Canadians be enriched by their example?

The contest, which ran from January until April 30, 1992, was limited to Aboriginal students or students of Aboriginal ancestry attending school. (*Aboriginal* as used here includes First Nations, Metis, Inuit, Treaty, Non-Treaty, Status, and Non-Status peoples.) Cooperating schools selected one winner in each category (grades K-3; 4-7; and 8-12) and forwarded those entries to Mokakit for final judging. Twenty winners were selected by the four judges.

In addition, entries were encouraged from students who wanted their writing considered, but were not interested in entering competitively. More than half the stories here were selected from those entries.

In addition to giving recognition to selected student writers, the book celebrates and praises the efforts of all the young writers from every corner of Canada who told us about their heroes. Thank you. Our hearts were touched by your beautiful stories.

Anita Ootoowak's illustration of the Transformer figure, Angakkugs.
(see page 46)

THE POWER OF STORIES AND STORYWORK

> In the old ways practised by many tribes, a person who is so inclined and capable on occasion sits and tells stories. The stories are woven of elements that illuminate the ritual tradition of the storyteller's people, make pertinent points to some listener who is about to make a mistake or who has some difficulty to resolve, and hold the listeners' attention so that they can experience a sense of belonging to a sturdy and strong tradition. (Allen, 1989, p.1)

> As with any generation
> the oral tradition depends upon each person
> listening and remembering a portion
> and it is together—
> all of us remembering what we have heard together—
> that creates the whole story
> the long story of the people.
> (Silko, 1981, p. 6-7)

> Stories, you see, are not just entertainment. Stories are power. They reflect the deepest, the most intimate perceptions, relationships, and attitudes of a people. Stories show how a people, a culture, thinks. (Keeshig-Tobias, 1990)

Each Aboriginal Nation has particular traditions and protocol concerning stories and the way that stories are to be told for teaching and learning purposes. The types of stories can vary from the sacred to the historical; from the development and perpetuation of the social/political/cultural ways to the personal life experiences and testimonials; and some are just for fun. Some stories may be "owned" or the responsibility of individuals, clans, or families; some belong to the "public domain," available for anyone to tell. In storywork, the context in which the story is used, the way the story is told, and how one listens to make meaning are as important as the story itself. The development and inter-relatedness of these elements make storywork fascinating and challenging.

When we asked for written submissions about Aboriginal Heroes, we left the genre to the discretion of the students. Many of the submissions were personal life experience stories. These stories focus on close family and community relationships and relationships to culture and to the land. Many Aboriginal people today tell personal stories to exemplify particular cultural teachings, to give criticism in what may be perceived as an indirect way, and to give encouragement to others. Often Elders will begin telling a life experience story when they are asked questions about cultural ways. Sometimes these personal stories are told along with traditional ones.

Some of the student writers submitted traditional/cultural stories and also stories which resonate with tradition which indicates that they are attempting to learn and carry on the oral tradition. To honour the good work of the students, we chose to focus on the use of stories and storywork for *Courageous Spirits*. Stories told and written from the form of the oral tradition can reflect a wholistic way of teaching and learning.

"Wholism" and Storytelling

The philosophical concept of wholism used in this book refers to the inter-relatedness between the **mind** (thinking), the **spiritual** (metaphysical values and beliefs and the Creator), the **emotional** (feelings), and the **physical** (body and behaviour/action) realms to form a **whole** healthy person. This development of wholism extends to and is mutually influenced by one's family, community, Band and Nation as shown by the diagram of concentric circles.

Included in the circle metaphor are the inter-relationships amongst the animal/human kingdoms, the elements of Nature and Land, and the Spirit World. Black Elk, holy man of the Oglala Sioux, reinforced these teachings about the circle:

> You have noticed that everything an Indian does is in a circle, and that is because the Power of the World always works in circles, and everything tries to be round. In the old days when we were a strong and happy people, all our power came to us from the sacred hoop of the nation and so long as the hoop was unbroken the people flourished. The flowering tree was the living center of the hoop, and the circle of the four quarters nourished it. The east gave peace and light, the south gave warmth, the west gave rain, and the north with its cold and mighty wind gave strength and endurance. This knowledge came to us from the outer world with our religion. Everything the Power of the World does is done in a circle. The Sky is round and I have heard that the earth is round like a ball and so are all the stars. The Wind, in its greatest power, whirls. Birds make their nests in circles, for theirs is the same religion as ours. The Sun comes forth and goes down again in a circle. The Moon does the same, and both are round.

> Even the seasons form a great circle in their changing, and always come back again to where they were. The life of a man is a circle from childhood to childhood and so it is in everything where power moves. Our tipis were round like the nests of birds and these were always set in a circle, the nation's hoop, a nest of many nests where the Great Spirit meant for us to hatch our children. (McLuhan, 1971, p. 42)

Ultimately the goal is to achieve some sense of mutualistic harmony or balance amongst all these parts. But there is often tension in this movement. Stories, especially the Trickster kind, help us to recognize these tensions and remind us about the need for respectful relationships or good inter-relatedness amongst the parts for achieving a sense of wholeness and wellness. Stories challenge the listener to think and imagine, allow the emotions to surface, provide opportunities for spiritual growth, and help to examine one's or others' behaviour or action.

Help From The Trickster

The *Trickster* theme has been used in *Courageous Spirits: Aboriginal Heroes of Our Children* to introduce the student authors and their cultural and geographical locations; to stimulate our imaginations and humour; to give clues about Aboriginal values, thought, and communication; and to show that unity can occur despite diversity. The Trickster theme provides an opportunity to discover the common understandings that exist amongst all peoples who live in a diverse country such as Canada.

The English word "Trickster" is a poor one because it cannot portray the diverse range of metaphorical meaning Trickster imparts to Aboriginal groups across Canada. Sometimes the Trickster is like a magician, an enchanter, prankster, like a Shaman, similar to a *brujo*, or sometimes a shape shifter. Trickster is a transformer figure, but one whose transformations carry good lessons using humour, satire, self-mocking, even absurdity sometimes.

In *Courageous Spirits* we have transformed Trickster (with the help of some of the student authors) into some of the characters and characteristics found in First Nations stories across Canada: Raven, Coyote, Wesakejac, Flint, Nanabozo, Glooscap, and others. In some places we introduce new kinds of transformations which the Trickster acknowledges as part of the contemporary context in which we now live. Trickster has lived since time immemorial and we assume she/he/it will live far into the future! Some of the student authors wrote about and drew their Tricksters. These submissions are found in the section "Trickster Storytelling For Teaching and Learning" which begins on page 42.

Just as each Aboriginal culture has particular ways of using storytelling, each culture has particular attributes and types of teachings connected to the Trickster. These may range from a character who is always getting into trouble by ignoring cultural rules and practices or by letting the negative side of "humanness" rule (such as vanity, greed, selfishness, and foolishness). Then Trickster subsequently learns lessons the hard way! On the other hand, Trickster has the ability to do good things for others and is sometimes like a powerful Spiritual Being and given much respect.

We hope that each school that uses *Courageous Spirits: Aboriginal Heroes of Our Children* will obtain the cooperation of cultural teachers and Elders to respectfully research their own cultural traditions, protocols, and practices for learning about and from the Trickster. We apologize for leaving out any Aboriginal Tricksters or for not re-presenting the Trickster in his/her/its full attributes.

A Trickster Story Begins....

In many Aboriginal cultures, the gifted storyteller starts the session of storytelling. We have asked Louise Profeit-LeBlanc who is a member of the Nacho N'y'uk Dun First Nation of the Northern Tutchone people of Mayo in the Yukon to share a Trickster story. Louise Profeit-LeBlanc is a well known storyteller who has learned the stories of her Ancestors. She carries out her cultural responsibility by teaching others through the oral tradition. Even though her story is written, it is shaped by the oral way of telling a story. Her Trickster story gives us, the educators/parents, many good things to think about regarding tradition, change, survival, and the processes of teaching and learning. Louise has given us permission to reproduce her copyrighted story.

The Native Indian Teacher Education Program (NITEP) of the University of British Columbia has kindly given us permission to reproduce their logo of Raven bringing light to the world, created by artist Phillip (Oppie) Oppenheim.

LOUISE PROFEIT-LEBLANC: STORYTELLER

RAVEN BRINGS THE LIGHT

"In the time of the end, young kids will speak like old people."

Smoke had filled the smokehouse where her Grandmother had been tanning hides. A pungent aroma of burning stumps, rotten to their core filled her nostrils. The air was electrified with rays of sunlight streaming through the planed walls with wire mesh, placed there to keep out the flies. These smoke filled rays were filtered with dying bugs gasping their last breaths, then slowly floating into the hot air streams of the smoldering wood. On the meat-cutting table, hornets staggered, overpowered from smoke inhalation; still taking in small bits of meat, as if to force their lives to continue.

"Be kind to hornets. They are the ones who kill the flies who spoil our meat with their maggots."

The Great Moose had once again given up its life for the people. Fresh meat for their stomachs. Hides for clothing and boats. Bones for tools. Nothing was wasted, not even its brains. The people used them for tanning moose hides. She could see her grandmother now swishing the "brain-bag" around in the tub filled with water. "Put your hand inside. When you can't see the palm of your hand anymore, then it is ready."

The old woman cupped her hand into the cloudy coloured water. The hide was ready now for its second soak. There was a science to this whole process. Breaking down the skin's fibres so eventually, after much scraping, soaking and evening out the thickness of the hide, it would become permeable. Once water could be squeezed through the hide, then it would be ready for smoking which made it even softer and more supple.

She didn't believe in doing only one thing at a time. Everything around her was interrelated. While the skin was soaking, she would cut meat in preparation for drying. Her knife was sure and accurate, separating, unfolding large chunks into flat sheets of flesh which would then be draped over poles lining the upper half level of the smokehouse. Ribs and moose brisket pieces hung in the corner becoming increasingly browner from smoke. An iron meshed grill held the teapot and a pot of boiling meat over the fireplace. Wiping the sweat from her brow with a piece of toilet paper she motioned to her granddaughter to join her now for a break. "Look around in that grub-box for a spoon and the sugar. There's some bannock in there too. And some jam."

She loved these times with her Gramma. There was so much to learn and she knew that her Gramma appreciated the help. She wondered if one day she would be as strong as her Gramma. A wet mooseskin could weigh up to at least 50 pounds. The way her Grandmother worked with it, it seemed so easy.

"Moose and camp-robber, they're related you know."

The old woman had cut pieces of meat and told her to place them outside the cache for them.

"You hear them? They're saying, 'Give me fat! I want fat!' That means that they will help you get a moose. They know how to call moose to you. You got to *feed them*!"

Since she could remember the young girl had been filled with many stories from her grandmother. Stories of the ancient past. Stories from another time, another world of existence. Stories of great courage, of transformation and trickery. Stories of great tragedies and struggles. Stories of grief and loss and resilience of a people who survived one of the most difficult environments for existence. Tales of wit and humour. She watched now as her grandmother took another sip of tea and lay back against the grub box. The spirit was charged and there was that familiar anticipation of another of these recollections. She leaned forward to listen ever more intently.

You know that's a spoiled kid, he's the one who helped to bring daylight to the world. He's the one who got the daylight, long time ago. Long time ago there was a Great Chief in the sky. He's the one, he owns the sun, the moon and all the stars. He's the one! He's got them all in His house in the sky. He's got a wife and a pretty daughter. Lots of men they like her, but her Daddy, he's very fussy, that time. He don't want just anybody to marry his daughter. He turn lots of guys away. Now Raven, he's flying around that time. He sees her too. He wish for her. But look how ugly he is. She won't even look at him. Just the same, he's going to try. He hears that girl ask her slave for water. Must be hot in that house!

She tell her, "Make sure you clean out that bucket really good, I don't want to drink dirty water." That slave woman she goes down to the creek, there. She rinse out that bucket four times. She don't know it! Raven he change himself into a little piece of dirt. He jump inside that water. Here that slave woman she take that water back. That young girl, she's pretty thirsty, and she just start to drink it fast. Here she choke that time.

"What for you give me dirty water? I thought I told you to rinse out that bucket good?"

"But, I did! I rinse it out four times. I don't see no dirt inside!"

Raven, he laugh to himself. He got inside of that girl now!

Well, not too long, here that woman she's started to get big. She's going to have a baby! Her Momma ask her when she been with a man.

"Where is that man now?" she asked her.

Her Daddy is sure mad about that. "Who's the Daddy?" He's pretty upset that time.

"I never been with nobody! I speak the truth. I don't know how I got baby inside me!" That young girl she start to cry, that time. She sure feel bad with her parents upset with her.

That baby he grow very fast inside her. He don't take long as baby takes. Just a few months. That girl, her mother she put down nice branches, clean caribou skin. She make it special for that baby to be born on top. That baby he got born quick. When that old woman clean him up, that baby boy he wink at her! She get shock.

"Why he do that to me?" she thinking.

That little boy he grows quick. Not even two months, here he walk around already. He talk good. That's the time he ask his Mommy to play with his Grampa's things. He like that sun. He want to play with it just like a ball, I guess.

"I don't think so!" she tell that to her boy. Here he sneak over to his Gramma. He ask her too.

"No, I don't think your Grampa he want to let it go, that one." That boy he just start to cry. He cry really hard! He cry so much that his eyes swell up. He can't catch his breath. Here he just about puke, he cry so much! His Grampa hear that boy and he feel sorry for him.

"Let him have it. He just gonna play with it inside house. It's okay!"

What a good time that little boy he have now. He just enjoy himself. He play around with that sun. He throw it around all year. He bounce it up and down. That's the one, he's Raven, you know. Pretty soon, when nobody gonna see him he pretend to get tired. That's the time the doors open. That sun he go right outside!

Heh! That man he's pretty mad now. That boy's Grampa. He bawl him out good.

"How come you let it go? That's my daylight, now it's gone. It disappear."

He let it go. He forget about it. He don't talk to that boy for long time.

Long time pass, that little boy he get kind of bored. He don't have anyone to play with that time. He's looking at the moon now. He wish for it. He start to cry again. He cry hard! Make himself sick again. He beg his Momma for it.

She tell him "No! Look what happened last time. That sun you let it go. Your Grampa he don't like that!"

That boy he don't give up. He go and cry some more to his Gramma. He know she going to spoil him. But her too, she say no to him. Now he really try hard to make them give it to him. This time he cry so hard, his eyes swell up, his nose running down, his stomach hurt. Can hardly have his voice, he cry so much! He choke too. Gee his Grampa feel sorry again.

"Give it to him!" He tell them womans to give that moon to that boy. He get happy right away. He play around with it. His Grampa tell again, "Don't lose this one grandson. I want you to take good care of it."

He don't know that's the one, he's Raven. Can't see it I guess!

So, just the same, those woman they watch, that Raven, he throw that moon up to window place. It's open. He pretends it's accident. Oh boy! Everyone really mad at him now!

"That's the last one you gonna get!" His Grampa holler really loud. His Grandmother and his mother they feel bad too. They don't think about that window, it's open for fresh air. It's hot in that house all the time.

Long time go by. Maybe one year, don't know. Again that little boy he want to play with something. He keep looking up there every day at his Grampa's things. He sees them stars up there. He wish for it. Here he not scared. He gonna try again. He start to cry for it. He say, "It's just accident, them other two. Daylight, I don't know it's gonna go out. Pleeeeease! Please!" He tell his Momma.

"I got nothing to play with. I wish for something." He start to cry again. "Give me the stars," he say. His Gramma and Grampa don't pay attention. His mother tell him, "Don't even think about it. Your Grampa, he's still mad at you, little one. You don't take care of his things. I know them twinkling stars you like them, but they belong to your Grampa and he's not going to give them to you!"

This time he sure know how to cry hard! Even worse than that first time. His eyes swell right shut, his lips all swollen up too. Red face that time. He throw up, everything. Pretty soon his nose start to bleed. Cry too much, that kid!

His Grampa can't stand it. He tell his wife, "Give it to him. Gee whiz, I don't like it for my grandson to be sick like that. You, you watch him good now. Don't let him lose stars next. Keep an eye on him. Watch door too!"

That boy he got really happy. He sure know how to make his Grampa feel sorry. Pretty soon he start to play around with it again. The stars, there's lots you know. He make them all tie up to one another, that time. He look. He saw his Grampa not there. His Gramma she sleep. His momma she busy, make grub for her father. He gonna come back soon. He went hunting that time, I guess.

He sneak! That time he's fast you know. Just open that door quick and stars go right out together! That boy, that's Raven, him too, he run out behind. He got the daylight now. Him, he going to bring it to the world, that time. He sure know how hey?

Smoke was beginning to get in the little girl's eyes, just as the story ended.

"Smoke always follows beauty," her grandmother said. "Time to get back to work now. You gonna bring in some more stumps for me? Gee, you sure are a good helper!"

This was a typical day in the life of a young First Nations girl who had the privilege of being raised partially by her grandmother. She was one of the few who had not yet been taken from her community to attend school. For the time being however, her classroom was the smokehouse and the curriculum being taught was life. She was being prepared for the future. Her mind was being taught to think on all levels and trained to understand things mentally but also emotionally and spiritually. Each concept of the stories was being heard by her heart.

"You got three ears you know. Two on the side of your head and one in your heart. Make sure you always use that one too!"

She remembered sharing this amazing phenomenon with her friends and they always tried to go with her to Gramma's place to hear the stories. They also liked the fact that each one of them understood the story how they were meant to understand it. No one was marked wrong in this classroom!

These heroes of early childhood gradually became blurred once in a regular school system which knew nothing of "Smokehouse Stories." There was a period of darkness, a period totally void of fantasy and the magic of mythological creatures and their adventures—these great super beings who were dauntless and were always able to meet any of the challenges that life placed before them. It was dark and so very quiet.

The Native voice was silenced across the land. Dark like the time before Raven stole the daylight. What she didn't realize was that despite the darkness and silence there was still activity in her mind. Activity of conceptual, intellectual development whose basis lay in those early teachings of her childhood. Memorization, analytical skills, recall, and oratory delivery were all deeply embedded and challenged her imagination and creative capacity to the maximum in private moments.

She longed to share the stories of her peoples' culture heroes and great speakers from the past and in high school wrote a comparative paper in English class. The teacher was not amused that she likened the great stories of her people to the Shakespearean tragedies. She did not see any relationship between Lady Macbeth and the woman whose greed overpowered her in the legend of the Blindman and the Loon. The young girl learned to remain silent amongst those who did not know. It was only her grandmother's voice that kept her in school until she finished, completely humiliated and demoralized for having to make excuses for her peoples' noble past. She always remembered her counsel when negative thoughts towards her teachers would come to mind.

"Every child is good when they're born. It's just the way others treat them that makes them turn out no good later on. Remember everybody has a little good in them, you just have to look for it. You gonna find it."

Now she understood what her grandmother had been saying so many years ago. We would have to look to every source of our culture, our ways to help the people during this time of healing. The stories would have to be remembered, and have to be shared again, particularly the stories of transformation and facing horrendous tests. These unimaginable feats would serve as a role model for this generation and the people would receive guidance and encouragement from the Ancestors who had gone on to the next world.

These life lessons would be too numerous to name but what is more important is that our children of today can be reassured that their future too, is great, and we have to bring our ancient knowledge to light and use it in our own lives, and share it with the rest of the world. Through this process there will be a realization that the most important hero to each one of us is the child within each of us: the child who throughout his or her own life is constantly like Raven trying to bring light to the world. Our responsibility as parents and educators is to ensure that each child becomes their true selves by attaining their full potential as human beings. In so doing, we will give birth to a far greater and nobler civilization than ever before.

May the Spirits of all the Grandmothers and Grandfathers who have gone on before us continue to assist us in this meritorious task of coming together as one Human Nation to sing the songs of all those special unsung heroes of the past, present, and of the future.

PURPOSES BEHIND THE BOOK

Four major objectives have provided direction for the development of *Courageous Spirits*. The first of these has already been referred to in the Introduction—to stimulate in First Nations children positive feelings about themselves and about their Aboriginal cultures.

The second objective is to provide First Nations schools with materials which are culturally relevant, and also to provide a process or model for producing their own culturally relevant materials.

The third objective is to promote storytelling as a culturally appropriate teaching/learning approach. Traditional storytelling is wholistic, and was and is used to convey information, examine values and behaviours, touch emotions, and explore cultural and spiritual concepts.

The fourth objective is to create awareness in public schools of Aboriginal cultures, communities, and cultural values through the stories in this book.

Some further practical considerations of these four objectives follow.

1. Culture and Self-esteem

The primary reason for developing this book has been to assist teachers (and others) to convey to Aboriginal children a positive sense of their cultural identity as Aboriginal persons in order to reinforce feelings of self-esteem.

The book presents a wide range of Aboriginal heroes from all walks of life, both historical and contemporary, high profile or "unknown," and from the four directions of Canada. We believe that children will find within these stories many personal points of reference that allow them to reflect positively on their culture and on themselves. The importance of positive messages which allow the individual to perceive inherent self-value cannot be overemphasized. Activities which assist students to reflect on personal meanings derived from these stories in order to build feelings of self-esteem are the recommended approach.

She remembered sharing this amazing phenomenon with her friends and they always tried to go with her to Gramma's place to hear the stories. They also liked the fact that each one of them understood the story how they were meant to understand it. No one was marked wrong in this classroom.

2. Culturally Relevant Resource Materials

The images and values which dominate the vast majority of books and materials used to teach Aboriginal children are based on European and mainstream North American cultures. Often, these materials are not relevant to the experiences of Aboriginal children.

This book provides stories written by Aboriginal children in their own settings, and reflects their experiences, feelings and values. Through rooting activities to cultural values, learning is likely to become more relevant and motivating than when such basic connections do not exist. By validating and valuing Aboriginal experiences and context, a message is being sent to the children that their culture is worthy and so are they. This sense of validation is, by and large, missing from mainstream curricular materials. . Moreover, by not validating Aboriginal children's experience, those children are given a negative message about their culture.

Research and writing activities can address other important culturally related values. These include reinforcing connections between children and their families, their community, with nature, with their schooling, and other connections which reflect Aboriginal values. These ideas will be explored further in later sections of this guide.

The use of the Trickster characters provide a unifying device for the many cultural groups represented in the book. This important figure may not be a familiar one to teachers or to their students. One section of this guide (beginning on page 42) is devoted to the Trickster in the hopes that both students and teachers will be motivated to learn much more about this fascinating character who has a parallel in all Aboriginal cultures.

A major principle guiding the development of culturally sensitive curriculum is to provide students with a sense of ownership as opposed to imposing ideas from the outside. Ownership has been accomplished in this book through the medium of the contest and non-competitive framework to provide student developed work. Although unified by the heroes theme, many other decisions were made by the individual writers, ensuring their ownership of the activity. These decisions include: topics, research approaches, writing forms (genres), revisions, and naming of the book.

Additional suggestions are provided throughout this guide to assist teachers to present the materials in a culturally appropriate way, and will, we believe, assist others to develop culturally sensitive materials of their own.

Now she understood what her grandmother had been saying so many years ago. We would have to look to every source of our culture, our ways to help the people during this time of healing. The stories would have to be remembered, and have to be shared again, particularly the stories of transformation and facing horrendous tests. These unimaginable feats would serve as a role model for this generation and the people would receive guidance and encouragement from the Ancestors who had gone on to the next world.

3. Storytelling as a "Wholistic" Teaching Approach

The importance of the story form to First Nations culture is of great significance. Stories contain images and messages which vividly convey values. They do so often with humour and in perhaps the most enjoyable of all "teaching" methods—is there anyone who doesn't love to hear a good story? Themes, characters, settings, and values portrayed in the stories are interrelated in subtle and sophisticated ways, and can be seen as the culture in microcosm. Because of the importance of the story form to First Nations teaching and learning, this topic has been expanded upon in two sections of this guide, one of which begins on page 1, the other on page 27.

...her classroom was the smokehouse and the curriculum being taught was life. She was being prepared for the future. Her mind was being taught to think on all levels and trained to understand things mentally but also emotionally and spiritually. Each concept of the stories was being heard by her heart.

"You got three ears you know. Two on the side of your head and one in your heart. Make sure you always use that one too!"

4. Creating Awareness About First Nations

The stories in *Courageous Spirits* offer teachers (whether in public or Band schools) an opportunity to create awareness about First Nations peoples, their cultures, their communities and their values as seen through children's eyes. Although there are many values held in common by all First Nations peoples—respect for nature, the land, all life forms—there are also many cultural differences. Many of these differences are shaped by geography—the Plains, the Coast, the Mountains, the Tundra, and now, the City. It cannot be assumed that Aboriginal children are knowledgeable about their local culture or about the cultures of other Aboriginal peoples. Through the stories presented in *Courageous Spirits*, a glimpse of various First Nations cultures is presented which portrays the diversity and parallels of "Aboriginalness" across Canada.

The stories need not be formally analyzed in order to communicate the cultural values they contain. Instead, the stories can be seen as offering a small window into the lives of the writers and their communities which is accessible to all. Most of the heroes that the students have chosen to write about are not obscure historical figures, but people who are "everyday heroes" with whom most children will have no difficulty identifying. The qualities the writers identify—kindness, sharing, courage, and leadership, among others—are readily apparent to most students.

An important issue in cross-cultural learnings is to accent similarities rather than differences. Many of the young writers have written with deep feeling about their heroes, and feelings know no cultural barriers.

As mentioned, geography has heavily influenced the ways in which all people have adapted their lives. All people develop a range of skills and behaviours for physical, emotional, spiritual and intellectual survival. Taken together, these behaviours and skills become a way of knowing the world, and knowing ourselves. The beliefs, behaviours, skills and knowledge form the bedrock of culture.

Children can readily appreciate the skills that have been developed and the intelligence which has been applied by peoples who have learned to adapt and thrive in Canada's diverse and often hostile climatic regions. Providing a brief setting for the stories can assist young readers to develop such appreciations.

Additional suggestions for achieving the objectives of creating awareness of Aboriginal cultural values can be found in the section titled *Seven Ways To Use This Book* (beginning on page 34).

> *...our children of today can be reassured that their future too, is great, and we have to bring our ancient knowledge to light and use it in our own lives, and share it with the rest of the world. Through this process there will be a realization that the most important hero to each one of us is the child within each of us: the child who throughout his or her own life is constantly like Raven trying to bring light to the world. Our responsibility as parents and educators is to ensure that each child becomes their true selves by attaining their full potential as human beings. In so doing, we will give birth to a far greater and nobler civilization than ever before.*

A FIRST NATIONS APPROACH TO TEACHING

This section expands upon the ideas presented in the Introductory section as well as introducing many approaches to using *Courageous Spirits* in the classroom. Our approach has been to suggest *strategies* rather than to develop individual lessons for each student's writing. Aboriginal stories usually contain many lessons. It is in this tradition that we have tried to honour the students' stories by presenting various ways for teaching and learning, with the anticipation that the teacher will select strategies appropriate to the learners and educational context.

There are four parts to this section:
1. Seven Concepts for Developing Cultural Sensitivity
2. Storytelling, "Wholism," and Teaching
3. Extended Family Grouping/Community Connections
4. Culturally Sensitive Research Techniques

1. SEVEN CONCEPTS FOR DEVELOPING CULTURAL SENSITIVITY

Both in terms of teaching for cultural sensitivity and for developing curricula for First Nations students, the following concepts can form a useful guiding framework: (1) a climate for non-threatening, non-judgmental participation, (2) provision for student ownership, (3) tapping imagination and emotion, (4) community and cultural relevance, (5) "factual" information on cultural practices and values, (6) individual uniqueness, and (7) the role of the teacher as a facilitator or guide.

Concept 1: Climate for encouraging participation

The essence of climate setting is embodied in the foundation value found in all First Nations cultures, that of *respect*. If respect for individual and group feelings, opinions, values, classroom contributions, and "personhood" are evident through the teacher's words, deeds, and body language, students are much more likely to feel inclined to participate more fully than they would otherwise, no matter what the topic at hand. Trust is developed.

Developing a respectful, encouraging climate rests largely on skillful interpersonal communication. Gazda, et al. (1984) have written extensively on this subject, albeit not in reference to First Nations peoples. Gazda's approach to communication skills is based on his concept of human development which relates to the whole person: the cognitive, physical-sexual, emotional, psycho-social, moral, vocational and ego modalities and their interrelationships. This wholistic approach is consistent with First Nations values.

Gazda is recommended reading because of the clarity of his vision of both the helping role and key components of the helping relationship, and because of the many exercises provided to help educators develop facilitative responding skills. Empathy, genuineness, respect, concreteness, self-disclosure, and appropriateness are some of the elements that Gazda emphasizes in the exercises to increase perceiving and responding effectiveness.

The goal is to establish a climate which facilitates the kind of responses which lead to healthy human development and growth. A facilitative climate is characterized by a relaxed and "emotionally honest" approach which casts the educator as a facilitator of learning in an atmosphere where each student feels safe and cared for.

Applications for *Courageous Spirits*

1. *The knowledge and practice of effective communication and facilitation skills will contribute to a climate in which students are more likely to participate. Such a climate is especially important for discussions of cultural values, but also for reviewing student written and oral work.*

2. *Detailed knowledge of cultural proprieties is very secondary to respectful, caring human interactions.*

> 3. *The recommended role of the teacher is that of a guide, a facilitator of learning, rather than a lecturer.*
>
> 4. *The use of "Talking Circles" (see page 35) and "Extended Family" activities (see page 30) are strategies for developing and extending participation of students, parents, and community.*

Concept 2: Student Ownership: Student-centred Learning

To engage students in genuine learning process, a curriculum which encourages a high degree of student ownership of learning seems most appropriate. Discovery learning, creative approaches, and a project emphasis all lend themselves to a high degree of participation and ownership. This concept places the student at the centre of the learning, and focuses on the needs of the student in contrast to the approach which sees the curriculum as the more important consideration.

A student-written and produced play which incorporates concerns which students have identified and researched would, for example, provide much more opportunity for student ownership (and *learning*) than would a lecture approach or teacher-led discussion on the same subject matter.

What is wanted are activities which challenge the higher intellectual abilities (analysis, synthesis, evaluation), provide opportunities for imagination, creativity, leadership and social interaction, and require students to take responsibility for their learning. Projects involving research and team efforts can offer these challenges.

Other examples of such approaches include school and community awareness activities such as production of a video or newsletter, a poster contest, school or community questionnaire, and student-arranged guest speaker series. Peer editing of written compositions works well if respectful foundations have been laid. Similarly, student evaluations of activities are valuable to building self-esteem and ownership.

The teacher's role is facilitative, leading brainstorming and planning sessions in the earlier stages, providing encouragement always, and advice when asked.

Applications for *Courageous Spirits*

1. *Cultural research projects which are student-directed are the activities of choice. These projects can be based on the themes around which* Courageous Spirits *is organized, such as determining local values in regard to honouring heroes, or interviewing Elders, or attitudes about hunting, for example. Students can work together in small groups or as a whole class group, although developmental leadership skills may need to be addressed in the earlier stages. Cooperative learning (its principles and practices) is a main teaching strategy that could be utilized.* Circles of Learning, *Johnson & Johnson (1984) is an excellent resource.*

2. *Students should make decisions about their topics for researching and writing. The sense here is not to abandon children who need guidance, but rather to facilitate their ownership of the topic. This may happen through prior classroom discussion and brainstorming, a dry-run of walking through the steps in selecting a topic, and so on. But in the end, the child/group should choose the topic to be explored, or decide whether to write a poem, play, story, or to produce a class newspaper.*

3. *Mokakit produced and distributed to Band schools across Canada "First Nations Freedom: A Curriculum of Choice (Alcohol, Drug and Substance Abuse Prevention) Kindergarten to Grade Eight." The section on "Projects" contains many ideas that may be adapted to* Courageous Spirits. *(See the final section, Related Reading, for information.)*

Concept 3: Tapping Imagination and Emotion

In general, cultural sensitivity requires that teachers recognize that learning occurs best through a careful blending of content (the ideas to be explored) and process (the structuring of the *way* the ideas are explored). It is not enough just to transmit information, although that is a necessary step. For that information to make a difference, to change learning behaviours somehow, then usually something more than transferring the information is needed.

Remembering to place the child at the centre of the learning helps here. Asking for feelings and reactions, engaging imagination and creative responses that in turn engage emotions can go a long way to make lessons come alive.

To illustrate the point: Rather than a fact-based approach such as *Fort Furtrader was founded in 1782 as a Hudson Bay trading post. Period. Move on to the next fact*, a series of questions can elicit more effective learning, for example:

What do you think it would have been like a) to witness the landing of a trading canoe setting up camp? b) to tell your parents about the arrival of a strange group of men in a canoe? c) to trap furs for trade? d) to bargain with the factor for your year's supply of furs? e) to help the strangers adapt to their new surroundings? f) to teach a child who doesn't speak your language how to play your favourite game? How would you *feel* if...? How do you think the (trappers, Aboriginal people, children) *felt* when...? What do you *think* would happen if...? And so on.

It is in the reactions and the emotions underlying them that we begin to learn about and to understand *the other* in a profound sense rather than in the more superficial sense provided by the neutral facts. To reach this level of interaction where learning of significance occurs, we often have to take a risk, to open up, to expose some vulnerability—but the climate has to be right, doesn't it?

To summarize, a subject area that has as a goal some degree of personal transformation (or why do we learn?) must take into account that feelings and attitudes are involved. Can true cultural understanding, for example, occur in a situation centred primarily on information giving?

Applications for *Courageous Spirits*

1. *Plan for a balance between the ideas you want to explore (content) and the way you go about exploring them (process). Plan activities that allow for creative expression, for expressing attitudes and feelings, for interpersonal transactions. Use examples from the book which show how the children described emotions.*

2. *During class discussions,* respectfully *invite answers which allow for expressions of feelings and attitudes in addition to those that provide information.* Thank you for sharing that story about your hunting experience. Would you be willing to tell us how you felt about shooting the rabbit?

3. *Allow time for processing feelings. Students may need time to think about how they feel. Silence in many First Nations cultures is a sign of respect. Silence allows time for good thinking.*

4. *As previously mentioned, students need to have an atmosphere where they can express their feelings without fear of criticism. The teacher must be able to discuss students' concerns and questions frankly in a climate based on trust. A facilitative approach is recommended.*

Concept 4: Community and Cultural Relevance

Many Band schools across Canada have been founded and administered by principles established in the 1972 *Indian Control of Indian Education Policy*, which was sanctioned as Federal Government policy in 1973 by Indian and Northern Affairs Canada. This educational policy is based on the two fundamental principles of *local control* and *parental responsibility*. Curricula which are adaptable to the local community students' culture, needs and interests are advocated. The employment of First Nations teachers and a program of cultural awareness activities for non-Native teachers are some of the recommendations.

The philosophical statement of the *Indian Control of Indian Education Policy* emphasizes the importance of education to promote self-esteem through cultural knowledge and pride:

> In Indian tradition each adult is personally responsible for each child, to see that he learns all he needs to know in order to live a good life....We...want our children to learn that happiness and satisfaction come from:
> - pride in one's self,
> - understanding one's fellowmen, and,
> - living in harmony with nature.
>
> We want education to give our children the knowledge to understand and be proud of themselves and the knowledge to understand the world around them. (National Indian Brotherhood, 1972, p. 1)

Embedding cultural values into education is also emphasized:

> We want education to provide the setting in which our children can develop the fundamental attitudes and values which have an honoured place in Indian tradition and culture....We believe that if an Indian child is fully aware of the important Indian values he will have reason to be proud of our race and of himself as an Indian. (ibid., p. 2)

Applications for *Courageous Spirits*

1. *If self-esteem is developed through cultural knowledge and values, then an individual will more likely practise respect (an essential value) for his or her person and toward others. Self-directed research on cultural themes can be a catalyst for developing self esteem,* particularly if the research includes as a primary goal establishing an educational relationship with community members.

2. *Efforts taken through whatever means to involve the local community education authority, parents, education workers, cultural centres, friendship centres and community members in cultural research projects will show that the school class is interested in and values community involvement and cultural knowledge. The wholistic approach to education encompasses all members of the learners' community. Local control of education is a two way effort requiring information flowing in both directions in regard to desirable goals and methods to reach those goals. Cultural research activities can be a pivotal process to connecting the school and the wider community.*

3. *The teaching methods should be appropriate, not contradictory to cultural ways of teaching and learning in any given community. Storytelling, modelling or demonstrating a skill or technique, using talking circles, and cooperative activities are only a few examples of traditional teaching approaches of First Nations peoples.*

4. *The seven principles outlined here have broad cultural relevance in all Aboriginal communities, but could form a basis for on-going discussion between educators and parents and local education authorities. Please refer to Mokakit's "First Nations Freedom: A Curriculum of Choice" for many more practical strategies.*

Concept 5: "Factual" Information on Cultural Practices and Values

There are several issues here, among them the appreciation of fact versus opinion, slanting of historical information depending on point of view and bias (Christmas dinner told from the point of view of the turkey?), varying accounts of the same event (the creation of the world), and so on.

What is important here is not that there are differences which cause discrepancies, but that those differences have reasons for existing. Even more important is a genuine respect for differences. What is not wanted is a levelling of differences to accommodate a common point of view. Rather, a position that accommodates ambiguity and diversity is recommended. My life is not better nor worse than yours, although each of us could make a case for either side. Life is complex. What is most important is the sense of wonder at life itself rather than wrangling over "facts" about life. An inquiry approach rather than a judgmental approach is recommended.

Applications for *Courageous Spirits*

1. Students can be taught how to assess the accuracy of information that they are exposed to. Students can learn the difference between facts and opinions; metaphor and reality; traditional values and contemporary interpretations. The issue is not one of right or wrong, good or bad, either/or. The issue is a search for cultural understanding through a realization that there are many truths, and that each culture—and individual—chooses its own. Many traditional stories promote the search for individual "truth" and understanding.

2. Students could compare the way that different student authors discussed cultural practices and values.

3. A comparison of the Native language and English could be used to show the difficulties in translation. For those familiar with Inuit syllabics, the one story included in Courageous Spirits in syllabics could be used to compare translation issues and differences between the Aboriginal and English languages. The issues such as the loss of humour in translation, and lack of precise words in English for the Aboriginal concept are issues that can be illustrated from stories in all Aboriginal languages.

4. Students could undertake a project which examines already published First Nations life experience stories in their own or other cultural areas. The focus of study could be to determine what information (factual and opinion) in regard to cultural practices is presented in the published works. The story told by Louise Profeit-Leblanc could be used as one example.

Concept 6: Individual Uniqueness

The central issue for cultural education programs for Aboriginal youth is probably to increase their understanding of *who they are* in regard to their Aboriginal culture. While some students will have a well developed sense, others may not have given it much thought or are avoiding giving it thought if the idea is emotionally volatile for them.

If behaviour change is seen as desirable in the context of cultural identity, that sense must be owned by the student. It is the student who must want to change, and seek ways of doing so. The analogy is that of an adoptive child who may or may not want to meet the birth mother. Efforts by others to impose change may be counter productive in the extreme.

The principle to be stated here is that each child comes with a unique gift. It is the role of others (educators, family) to help each child to recognize and value his or her uniqueness.

> *Every child is good when they're born. It's just the way others treat them that makes them turn out no good later on. Remember everybody has a little good in them, you just have to look for it. You gonna find it.*

Applications for *Courageous Spirits*

1. The stories in this book resonate with the young writers' feelings about their culture. Many of the stories will cause young Aboriginal students to reflect on their own feelings about their heritage. Respectful encouragement to explore such feelings can assist students in their search for their "sense of self." Often overcoming difficult problems helps one come to know and appreciate "self."

2. Perhaps some of the best teaching and learning that occurs falls outside the regular curricular objectives. Helping children to understand their uniqueness and their "gifts" and offering reassurances of self-worth can be the most valuable contributions a teacher can make to a child's education.

Concept 7: The Teacher's Role

Throughout the preceding discussions, the teacher's role has been emphasized. All teachers have the power and capacity to set a climate which will encourage participation, to provide opportunities for student ownership, to tap imagination and emotion, to provide community and cultural relevance to the learning, to help students understand apparent factual/cultural ambiguities, and to help children gain a sense of their uniqueness.

The approach which has been recommended throughout this exploration of teaching concepts for cultural sensitivity is that of a facilitator, a guide to learning.

The facilitator facilitates; that is, *makes easier* using the original sense of the word. The role of the teacher can be seen as helping to ease communication, problem solving, interacting, planning, learning.

Facilitators prefer to *guide* the learning, rather than control it. They assist the students to control their own learning. They often don't provide answers, but instead help students to learn how to find the answers for themselves. They assist students to take control of their lives rather than trying to control the students' lives.

For many teachers, the role is already a familiar one. Others might find it daunting. The suggestions in this book might help teachers to explore or refine this recommended approach.

2. STORYTELLING, "WHOLISM," AND TEACHING

Since she could remember the young girl had been filled with many stories from her grandmother. Stories of the ancient past. Stories from another time, another world of existence. Stories of great courage, of transformation and trickery. Stories of great tragedies and struggles. Stories of grief and loss and resilience of a people who survived one of the most difficult environments for existence. Tales of wit and humour. She watched now as her grandmother took another sip of tea and lay back against the grub box. The spirit was charged and there was that familiar anticipation of another of these recollections. She leaned forward to listen ever more intently....She was being prepared for the future. Her mind was being taught to think on all levels and trained to understand things mentally but also emotionally and spiritually. Each concept of the stories was being heard by her heart.

*"You got three ears you know. Two on the side of
your head and one in your heart. Make sure you
always use that one too!"*

Jo-ann: The story and life experiences of Louise Profit-LeBlanc
resonate with my experiences of learning about the uses of
storytelling for teaching and learning. For a long time the traditional
stories of our Ancestors were put to "sleep" (as the Sto:lo Elders
have said), and not considered as important tools for learning. Our
stories have undergone major transformations from the Aboriginal
language to English; and from the oral delivery to the print and visual
media. Often the humour and depth of meaning has been lessened,
especially with the language differences. Despite the major
problems of these transformations, many of the stories and their
essence have survived and we are fortunate to be able to hear and
read about the voices of Aboriginal storytellers today. Today many
more Aboriginal people are becoming involved in reactivating the
use and the form of storytelling in various media.

Life experience stories are also being recognized as important ways
to pass on cultural teachings and knowledge, and to give listeners
hints on becoming good human beings. People who share these
stories have usually experienced various hardships and want others
to learn from their experiences—a common traditional practice.

With stories I have learned that it is important to be able to have
enough patience to listen with "three ears," to go away and think
deeply about the meanings of the story. My friend Richard
Wagamese said we need to "take the story away and find our own
truth in it."

With storywork I have learned that it is important to understand the
metaphors and symbolism used in the stories. Traditional Aboriginal
stories contain many symbolic forms such as the use of the number
four (four seasons, phases of life, cardinal directions), the circle, and
particular animals (such as the rabbit, which may have powers like a
medicine person).

I have also learned how important it is to hear a story over and over
again. As the listener-learner ages, new layers of meaning are
uncovered.

Beginning The Circle With Stories

Many Aboriginal stories are a continuation from a previously told
story or theme. The Trickster journeys are an example in which the
meanings from these stories build upon each other; yet the story can
also stand alone. One can enjoy and learn from one story, but when
the story is understood in relation to the whole (culture or group),
then even more understandings are gained. The stories in

Courageous Spirits are like that. An appreciation can be gained from each person's writing; yet put together in a collection such as this book, a deeper understanding emerges of Aboriginal people and their cultures.

We recognize that bringing the mind, the spiritual, the emotional, and the physical realms together in mutualistic harmony is challenging to say the least. Wholism is a goal which we advocate because there is so much healing to be done in Aboriginal families and communities as a result of assimilationist assaults on our cultures. Wholism as we understand it is the essence of a traditional way of life. If we are to become whole, healthy people and Nations, then we must address the mind/spiritual/emotional/physical development and interactions. The process of addressing wholeness can vary and is as important as knowing the parts. Sometimes one area needs more attention than others. Sometimes some areas converge for particular reasons, other times they do not. The important consideration is knowing the parts and working at bringing them together for wellness.

A story or a combination of stories can help us to focus on particular areas. Just as each person has a place around the circle, each story can contribute to the circle of wholeness.

Applications for *Courageous Spirits*

1. An introductory framework for wholism could use the following questions or guiding comments:

Mind *(thinking). What have I learned? What can I imagine? What do I think?*

Spiritual *(metaphysical values and beliefs, the Creator). Understanding that everything has a spirit—a being. In Aboriginal stories there are numerous transformations (such as people turning into rocks or animals and vice versa) which show inter-relatedness and which acknowledge that each thing has a spirit. What is my relationship to the Creator? (or whatever name or religion is appropriate to the school context).*

Emotional *(feelings) What do I feel?*

Physical *(body and behaviour/action) How can I take good care of my body? What will I start, stop, and/or continue to do?*

2. *Plan the parts of your individual lessons in the framework of the whole. Considerations of process as well as content are essential to achieving wholistic goals. Where possible, relate one activity to another.*

3. *A regional cluster of stories, such as the ones from Alberta, may be used to identify ways students wrote about learning, feeling, being/Spiritual, and action. Particular stories may be used to highlight certain aspects of wholism. This kind of analysis could be extended to local cultural stories.*

4. *A language/language arts/English study may be introduced on metaphor and symbolism in Aboriginal traditional stories. Comparisons between the Native language and the English language could be begun, in particular, any concepts in which one language does not have a parallel. How these differences affect meaning could be discussed.*

3. EXTENDED FAMILY GROUPING/COMMUNITY CONNECTIONS

Two major concepts are offered here. The first has to do with moving away from age/grade groupings and moving towards more culturally related groupings. The second extends that thought by moving beyond the school and connecting with the community.

In order to reinforce traditional family values in the school setting, the suggestion here is to move away from the usual age/grade groupings, and instead encourage groups of varying ages to work together.

Just as subjects can be connected, so can children of different ages and grades, although in many schools, some extra efforts might have to be made.

It should be possible in most schools to arrange for a set time each day or week, for example, for a grade seven student to work with one or more younger students, simply to read to them or listen to them read, or to ask them spelling words, or to help them write a story or a letter, or to help with an art, science, or social studies project.

The benefits are many. As well as giving responsibility to the older student, this method also builds self-esteem. The older student may be motivated to improve his or her own learning skills as a result of the new role model responsibilities built into the helping role taken on. The benefits to the younger students are an increase in individualized attention—that is, caring—and a young mentor and role model. The benefits to the teacher are increased time for working with individuals or small groups who need special attention.

This suggestion may be nothing new to teachers who work in ungraded or multi-graded classrooms. For Aboriginal and most other students, it is a natural extension of family ties and community values.

Beyond this suggestion is that of bringing in community members to work in similar constellations. Parents and grandparents, aunts and uncles, older brothers and sisters, helping, caring, connecting the classroom to the community.

This connection with the community is strengthened through inviting adults from the community to become involved as speakers, demonstrators of cultural skills and knowledge, volunteer classroom tutors, home-school committee members, and so on.

How can these ideas work for you?

Applications for *Courageous Spirits*

1. The older student can read the stories to the younger ones, re-read favourite stories, or listen to the younger ones read.

2. The helper can assist the younger ones to make up their own stories based on ideas suggested by the Courageous Spirits stories, simply listen to the younger children talk about their related experiences, or answer their questions.

3. They can help the younger students write their stories down, suggest ways to illustrate them, help with their spelling, and so on.

4. Community storytellers can be invited to tell their stories (every Friday afternoon?)

4. CULTURALLY SENSITIVE RESEARCH TECHNIQUES

Here is a brief approach to thinking about culturally sensitive research. A decision to do some research means not only thinking about the topic, but also about the sensitivities of people who are the focus of the research. The challenge is to do serious inquiry (research) in ways that do not oppose cultural values and practices.

This approach includes both areas of consideration through asking a series of questions during planning sessions. Some suggestions are offered here.

(1) Considerations for Planning and Doing Research:

(a) Framing the Research Question

- **What** is the purpose of this research? (**What** benefit will it have to me/school/community? **Why** is it important?)

(b) Getting the Research Information

- **How** was serious inquiry about a topic (research) traditionally/culturally practised?
- **How** will I gather the information? **What** kind of research techniques will I use? (i.e., identify and examine historical, written and oral sources; interviews, questionnaires). **Where** can I find this information? **Who** can I ask? **Why** is this the most appropriate method to use?

(c) Analyzing the Information/Conclusions

- **What** will I do with the information? If I use an interview or questionnaire, **how** will I summarize the major themes and messages?
- **What** have I learned from my research gathering?

(d) Re-presentation of research findings

- **Who** must I check back with (*all* the people I interviewed) to ensure that I have correctly portrayed their ideas/knowledge?
- **How** will I share this information with my class, school, and/or community? (Oral or written report, video, play, poster, panel discussion, debate, ???)

(2) Ethical Considerations

(a) Respect

- **How** can I do respectful research so people are not hurt? (respect for people, respect for cultural knowledge)
- **What** are the cultural protocols/practices that I should follow? (a certain way of asking for help, giving a gift, following a traditional practice)

ETHICS CHECK: Have I been respectful in my treatment of people and their feelings, and in following cultural practices?

(b) Confidentiality

- **What** material must be kept confidential? (People have a right to feel that their identity will be kept anonymous if they so wish. Their information will be shared with others, but connecting their statements to their name will not be done unless they agree.)

ETHICS CHECK: Have I given assurances to people that their identity will be kept anonymous if they so wish? Have I kept my word?

(c) Verifying information

- **Who** should verify my work? (It is important that the information people have provided especially through interviews is presented accurately. These people may also want to add or change information once they see it in print. It is therefore essential to verify your work with *everyone whose information you use.*)

ETHICS CHECK: Have I brought the printed information from my analysis back to the people who told it to me (for their approval)?

5 W-H

A useful way to generate questions is to ask ourselves:

Who, What, Where, When, Why, and How

SEVEN WAYS TO USE THIS BOOK

Seven suggestions for using this book with students are provided here in the hopes of stimulating further creative uses both at school and at home. These are:

      (1) writing themes
      (2) research and question raising
      (3) talking circles
      (4) cultural studies
      (5) integrated studies
      (6) Trickster storytelling for teaching and learning
      (7) reading for enjoyment.

(1) Writing Themes

The writing theme which produced this book was that of Aboriginal Heroes. The students' stories contain many additional themes: the importance of family, traditional teachings, personal accomplishments, devotion, adventure, sharing, caring, leadership, sacrifice, cultural activities, inspiration, careers, sports, sorrow, hunting, music, cooperation, spirituality, and others.

It is often difficult for students to write about such abstract topics. What is helpful is for them to read or hear stories to stimulate their thinking about a particular theme or topic. A helpful teacher's role is to provide the initial stimulation and to guide the writing process. The stories in this book can be used to illustrate the sub-themes which have been chosen and written by children.

By first listening to the stories, and with some initial guidance, children can learn to identify story themes. They can generate ideas in a small group, and choose one of the themes or one of their own to write about. The book works well as a catalyst to stimulate the imagination as a starting point for writing.

Applications for *Courageous Spirits*

Because of the importance of the writing themes concept, a Theme Unit on Aboriginal Heroes is included as a separate section of this guide (page 63).

(2) Research and Question Raising

An essential part of the education process is for children to learn how to raise questions. Formal reading for comprehension exercises are nearly entirely based on questions and answers. "Research" is about raising and answering questions, nothing more intimidating than that.

By learning to ask *who, what, why, where, when* and *how* questions, students are given a simple tool to begin the writing and researching process.

The section on *Culturally Sensitive Research Techniques* (page 32) elaborates on culturally sensitive research.

The stories in this book can help with the writing and research process. The teacher's role is initially to raise questions to help students think about the story, and to help students learn how to raise their own questions. What is not wanted here is a tedious exercise, but rather a few questions to assist students to develop their insights. The question raising can lead directly to a related writing activity.

Applications for *Courageous Spirits*

Community and cultural resources teachers could help the group learn respectful ways of asking questions to Elders. Often the "who, how" question may not be appropriate. Also, students should be prepared to wait "patiently" for an answer.

(3) Talking Circles

The Talking Circle is recommended as a teaching strategy consistent with First Nations values. The circle is a powerful symbol of connectivity and completeness. The circle is the earth, the sky, the sun, the moon, the tipi, the seasons, the cycle of life.

The Talking Circle has long been a place where everyone is equal, where all can have a say. It is a healing circle where the heart can be unburdened, and words of consolation can be freely spoken. In many First Nations contexts today, the Talking Circle concept is used mainly for emotional healing purposes, although the Circle is not exclusively for this purpose.

In the classroom Talking Circle, children can learn to listen respectfully, and to express their ideas (if the right climate prevails) without fear of ridicule. Since silence and long pauses carry different messages in different cultures, it could be very helpful to include an Elder or others knowledgeable in cultural ways to facilitate the introduction and use of Talking Circles in the classroom.

A talking stick, feather, or a stone can be held by the speaker to signal that it is she or he who now has the right to speak, and the others have the responsibility to listen. Often these objects are reminders of our connection to the land and to respectful cultural values. Children who may ordinarily interrupt or demand inordinate attention can learn to listen respectfully until it is their fair turn to speak. Those who may not normally participate may overcome their reticence in the safety of the respectful Talking Circle.

Usually what is said is left at the Talking Circle or absorbed by the object passed around. In this way, children learn not to "spread rumours" about what was said.

It is in the Talking Circle that children can develop confidence in presenting their views, exchanging ideas, examining concepts, raising questions, and exploring ideas. These are some of the activities which we would encourage to help children consider the themes, values, and emotions found within the stories in *Courageous Spirits* and in related writing activities which might follow.

Learning to respect and appreciate differences between groups is a legitimate and necessary classroom activity. *Courageous Spirits* offers the content to provide many opportunities for such learning. The Talking Circle provides an appropriate framework for those lessons.

Applications for *Courageous Spirits*

1. *The group (students, teacher, cultural teacher) should decide upon the purposes and name of the Talking Circle. The ways (norms, rules, cultural practices) of listening and speaking need to be agreed upon and developed.*

2. *Many Talking Circles begin with a prayer or "opening words" to create the readiness for the work of the circle. Many of our Elders say these thoughts help "to clear the mind, open the heart, and connect us with each other and the Creator."*

3. *Selections from Courageous Spirits could be used as a focus to begin a discussion. Perhaps one of the "characters" experienced a problem that others in the group are experiencing. Identifying with the character or the situation or the solution is usually less threatening.*

4. *Individual students of the same classroom or from another grade could learn to become facilitators of the Talking Circle discussion.*

(4) Cultural Studies

Many suggestions can be found throughout this Guide for using *Courageous Spirits* to create cultural awareness about Aboriginal peoples, and so this section may appear to be somewhat redundant or obvious.

However, we would like to introduce here a point of view specifically about cultural studies and cultural awareness programs, and the implications for using *Courageous Spirits* as part of a cultural studies program.

The two writers of this Guide have also produced a workshop guide entitled *Creating Cultural Awareness About First Nations (1992)* for the Native Indian Teacher Education Program, University of British Columbia and the BC Ministry of Education. The following excerpt from that guide has been slightly reworked to fit the present context:

> We believe that cultural awareness programs which have focussed on "beads and feathers" have had questionable impact or relevance to the education of First Nations children. If the awareness has remained focussed on the beads and feathers alone without inter-relating cultural

values and knowledge embedded in the cultural material forms, there is a danger of "artifact stereotyping."

The same could be said about using traditional stories. When the stories have been improperly brought into the mainstream setting such as schools, it is common that either their meaning has been misunderstood or their significance has gone unrecognized resulting in the cultural lesson being denigrated to a "simple tale." This is because the physical, material components of culture are somewhat empty without the emotional, spiritual, attitudinal, and intellectual underpinnings which have produced them.

The important territory here is the *values* embedded in the objects and stories, not necessarily the surface image of the objects and stories, which may be quite beautiful in themselves. This creates a problem for cultural awareness programs since it takes a long time for the relationships between the material objects and values within them to begin to emerge, let alone to be understood or fully appreciated. Without cultural context, the wholistic relationships are missing and a piecemeal approach to teaching about First Nations culture will most likely occur.

Cultural awareness programs are likely to be more successful in attaining the goals set for them if more emphasis is placed on **providing opportunities for people to interact**. Stories, art, and objects can be used as a way of promoting interactions between people, but they must be used in ways which ensure that some broad understandings of the values that drive the culture are raised to a conscious level. This is not readily done, and the process is not unlike that of learning a new language. Slowly, slowly the new words and grammatical forms fall into place.

As a caution, we suggest that there are no "quick fixes" through cultural awareness programs. People who want fast answers to very complex questions often become impatient because they cannot understand why you are talking about Aboriginal fishing rights when all they really want to know is why Jimmy is always coming late and Nellie never answers in class.

The point here is that cultural understanding is a very complex concept, and one that requires an approach that sees both the forest and the trees. A recommended approach encourages a sense of the marvel of it all—the value of the total ecology—and gives less emphasis to studying the names of the trees or trying to figure out the reason why birch trees have white bark and cedar trees have reddish brown. The wholistic approach will emphasize relationships and understanding, and find ways to draw awareness to those things that humans share, and find joy in the diverse expression of the many human patterns that we call culture.

It is in the spirit of those thoughts that we suggest *Courageous Spirits* as a springboard to cultural studies.

Applications for *Courageous Spirits*

1. *Traditional teachings are practices, values, or beliefs that are passed from generation to generation. Students could identify examples of traditional teachings found in the Heroes selections. An example of a traditional teaching such as respect for the land could form the core of a webbing activity which shows the inter-relationships between people, practices, environmental knowledge, and contemporary environmental issues.*

2. *The role of the Elders as teachers could be discussed and the way that Elders teach the younger people could be examined.*

3. *First Nations language names/words could be charted and cultural area identified.*

4. *Further study on the role and responsibilities of the local Chief and Band Councillors could be undertaken.*

5. *Examples of cultural changes could be explored with these guiding questions: What created cultural change? How were the people affected? How did the Heroes help the students, their families, or communities overcome cultural change? Students should come to realize that all cultures change over time. Some traditional principles, in particular values and beliefs such as respect for the land and Elders, have continued to exist. Students could also discuss and chart the positive and negative effects of cultural change.*

6. *Students could identify the local storytellers and find out the appropriate cultural way of inviting the storyteller to their class. In preparation, cultural protocol should be researched (gift, food, how one listens, does one ask questions?). Parents, teachers, community members, and students could collect the written and audio-visual story sources that exist in either their local region or in their province/territory.*

7. *A regional cultural study could be introduced by using a group of students' stories. For example, the authors from the Northwest Territories introduce themes of connection to the land, influence of climate/geography, Inuk names, culture change, Spiritual beliefs, and contemporary cultural context. Their work can be used to bridge to various subject concepts/skills.*

(5) Integrated Studies

Some suggestions follow for integrating *Courageous Spirits* into the general curriculum.

WRITING:
A full section dedicated to using *Courageous Spirits* as the basis of a writing unit is included in this Guide beginning on page 63.

ENGLISH/LANGUAGE ARTS:
Appropriate activities include using *Courageous Spirits* stories for:
- critical thinking issues
    - facts vs. opinions
    - persuasion, coercion, bias, etc.
    - debating and its rules
    - criticism, reviews,
- research skills:
    - library skills
    - narrowing a topic
    - report writing
    - oral reports
- journal writing
- letter writing
    - for information
    - invitations to speakers, etc.
    - thank you notes
- school newspaper
    - reporting
    - editing
- personal writing
    - poems
    - essays
    - dramatic scripts
    - descriptive language
- literature
    - First Nations writings
    - general literature on related topics
- biography

FINE ARTS:

Art, drama, dance, and music can all accommodate activities related to *Courageous Spirits*, from creative production through to performance. Plays for radio, stage, and video production can incorporate many of the fine arts in collaboration.

- posters, illustrations of the stories
- script writing: write a Trickster play
- performance
- video and theatre production skills
- scenery and props
- interpretive dancing
- musical accompaniments, song writing
- introduce the music of Kashtin, Susan Aglukark, Buffy Sainte Marie

HISTORY:

- the history of First Nations people in a given area
- the history of European contact
- important leaders

SOCIAL STUDIES:

Many possibilities arise from the stories, such as:

- map making
  - map the location of the various stories
  - map the Tricksters' journeys
- geography of the story locations
- industries, jobs, resources, etc., in those locations

Some of the themes and issues lend themselves to research units, such as:

- self-government issues
- issues of land claims
- alcohol and drug abuse
- family tree projects

MATHEMATICS:

- measuring Trickster's journey, estimating
- use Trickster character to make math fun, create and solve problems
- counting in a First Nations language
- graphs of the kinds of Heroes portrayed

SCIENCE:

Environmental studies can easily be coupled with themes found in many of the stories in *Courageous Spirits*—including survival, respectful harvesting of natural resources, seasonal migrations, etc. What did some students learn about medicinal plants? (NOTE: some plants have to be carefully used and can be dangerous if not used correctly.) How did students' environments affect their lifestyles?

CAREERS:
- draw awareness to the diversity of careers, jobs (such as artist, mechanic, teachers, journalist, carver, singer, activist, storyteller, model, lawyer, homemaker, chief, actor, business, etc.)
- have students research the preparation and education, roles and responsibilities, etc. required for these careers.

HEALTH:
The life stories as told from the viewpoint of the student could be used to introduce issues of alcohol abuse, teen pregnancy, low self-esteem, family problems, and other concerns. The important consideration is that these students and their families found ways to overcome some of the problems associated with these issues. Their story is shared to give hope and encouragement to others who may feel alone with their problems.

(6) Trickster Storytelling For Teaching and Learning

The *Trickster* has been used in *Courageous Spirits: Aboriginal Heroes of Our Children* to introduce the student authors and their cultural and geographical locations; to stimulate our imaginations and humour; to give clues about Aboriginal values, thought, and communication; and to show that unity can occur despite diversity. The Trickster theme provides an opportunity to discover the common understandings that exist amongst all peoples who live in a diverse country such as Canada.

In *Courageous Spirits*, we have transformed Trickster (with the help of the student authors) into some of the characters and characteristics as found in First Nations stories across Canada: Raven, Coyote, Wesakejac, Flint, Nanabozo, Glooscap, and others. Some of the student authors wrote about and drew their Tricksters. Four of these submissions follow the *Applications* section below.

Additional comments about the Trickster are found in an earlier section of this Guide (beginning on page 4).

Applications for *Courageous Spirits*

1. *Using the research section's guidelines, students could research the cultural tricksters in their stories. Four student examples are provided below which could be used as examples for learning more about the various characteristics of Trickster. The research could extend to characters other than transformers who help teach cultural rules or behaviours (such as in the fourth story which follows).*

2. *Securing the support and cooperation of local cultural resource teachers and Elders is essential before having students do cultural research. Sometimes the stories and characters may have strong spiritual significance and may not be appropriate for particular levels of children.*

3. *Louise Profeit-LeBlanc's story (page 5) should be read orally to the students. Her story contains many teachings and themes which could be discussed:*
   - *how the Gramma taught her granddaughter*
   - *inter relatedness*
   - *stories for strength, healing*
   - *metaphor and symbolism of light and darkness*

4. *Trickster can be helpful with discipline: what gets us into trouble and how can we learn from our mistakes?*

FOUR STUDENT ARTICLES ABOUT THE TRICKSTER CHARACTER

"WESAKEJAK"

by Shylo Jones

Wesakejak is a trickster for the Ojibway and Cree people, or, as they call themselves, the Anishiniwak.

Wesakejak can shape shift to any animal or spirit form.

Elders tell young people stories or legends about Wesakejak and when the world was different than we know it today. The Anishiniwak and the animals, birds and other creatures lived together, talked the same language and shared everything.

Wesakejak represented both good and evil. He helped life and other things become as we know them today. He would also play tricks on humans and animals. For example, his stories explain how the beaver got his flat tail, why the goose waddles when he walks, how the snake lost his legs and why we have different seasons.

Wesakejak also helped other people fight the bad spirits like the Windigo. The Windigo made people do bad things to each other. Wesakejak was only human and he needed the Thunderbird Spirit's help to fight the Windigo.

The legends of Wesakejak are told to children of all ages to teach them how this world was formed and why we should respect all the children of Mother Earth because they all have a role to play in this world.

Illustration of Wesakejak by Shylo Jones

"NANABOSHO"

by Quin Kirkness

Nanabosho was a great teacher. He was also a helper. He brought corn and fire to the people so that they could have food and warmth, for example.

He was the son of the West Wind and the grandson of the Moon. He was magic and could take different shapes. Sometimes he liked to trick people to get things for him or his people.

You can say and spell his name different ways. Nanabosho and Nanabush are two of the ways that his name is said by the Ojibway people of Ontario and Manitoba. The Ojibway people from around Sault Ste. Marie that told stories about Nanabosho came to Manitoba in the early 1800's. They kept on telling their children about Nanabosho for generations and generations. These stories are still told by the Saulteaux and Ojibway people in Manitoba, and probably Ontario, today. When stories are being told by the Ojibway people, Nanabosho's spirit lives on. They remember this spirit by saying "Bosho" when they greet each other.

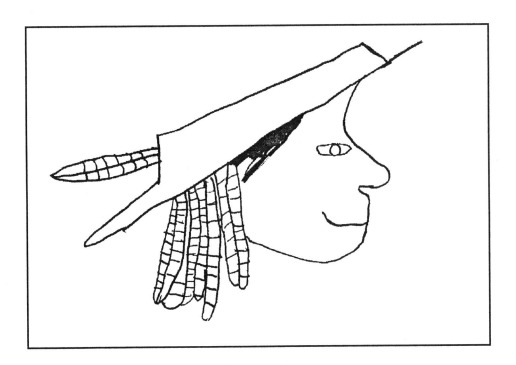

Illustration of Nanabosho by Quin Kirkness

"ANGAKKUGS"

by Anita Ootoowak

Angakkug is the Inuktitut word used for a shaman or a man with magical powers. There were many Angakkugs on Baffin Island in the past and Inuit were in great awe of them because of their magical powers. People living in the small camps were afraid if they did not do what the Angakkugs told them as bad luck might then befall the camp and people would die. The Angakkugs often became leaders because of their power and trickery. They wore many amulets or charms which helped them to call on the spirits to act for them. Angakkugs were both good and bad. Before medical help was available in the north, Angakkugs acted as doctors healing the sick and trying to save the dying, but some would also cause the death of people who disobeyed or were not liked by them. Others would claim to be able to travel great distances to other lands or even the moon and lead their camp groups over miles of land to new hunting grounds. Many claimed to be able to change people or objects into animals thereby threatening people who did not follow any of the taboos of the Inuit camp.

I learnt more about Angakkugs after seeing the movie "The White Dawn" which is based on the book written by James Housten. In the story, which is based on fact, the Angakkug plays an important role. In the early 1900's three stranded whalers were helped to survive the long dark winter by a group of Inuit camped on south Baffin Island. However, when the hunting became bad and people hungry, the Angakkug cleverly put the blame on the visitors finally causing their death.

With the arrival of the Christian missionaries to the North, the power of the Angakkug gradually became less and less. Inuit, converted to Christianity, no longer respected the Angakkugs and were not afraid of their trickery. Early missionaries said they were "evil spirits" and people should not talk or go near to them. Their relatives, however, still survive today.

More recently there is a renewed interest in Angakkugs, but as historical figures not as the Trickster with magical powers as before.

"QALLUPILLUIT"

by Samson Ootoowak

A Qallupilluq is an imaginary Inuit creature which has had many stories told about it that have now become legends. Alone or in groups, the Qallupilluit swim in the icy sea water and appear often in ice cracks or at the floe edge. They watch for people, especially children who are too close to the edge, and will suddenly grab them pulling them down into the deep cold water never to be seen again. As many Inuit live on the coast, especially on Baffin Island, children often play on the ice and long to jump the cracks in spring time. The story of the Qallupilluq was told to children in order to scare them away from the dangerous cracks and ice floe edge.

In many stories, the Qallupilluq has a human but rather ugly face, and a fish tail similar to a mermaid's. It usually has long shaggy hair and sometimes a covering of feathers or a parka.

Illustration by Samson Ootoowak of a Quallupilluq

(7) Reading For Enjoyment

Finally, the stories in *Courageous Spirits* can be read for pleasure just as they are, and for what they are, the creative writings of young Aboriginal people.

BEYOND *COURAGEOUS SPIRITS*...

By Peg Klesner

Throughout this collection of writings about Aboriginal Heroes the Native student authors have expressed their knowledge and personal belief in the primary values of their respective cultures. This has occurred naturally, without prompting, resonating from the very centre of their family and community experiences.

These values, surviving over hundreds of generations, and vital to survival in traditional times, have also survived the recent destructive forces of residential schools, miseducation, assimilation pressures, welfare apathy, alcohol abuse, urbanization, etc.

There is a great need for many Native students to have exposure to culturally relevant material which broadens their individual life view. These experiences can provide a growth in self esteem through the mirroring effect of examining their own cultural roots while gaining strength from shared viewpoints.

Mythology as Education

In the section titled "The Power of Stories and Storywork," explanation is given about the purposes and uses of storytelling for passing on the teachings and belief systems from one generation to another. This process was formalized within local communities as potential storytellers (cultural historians) were thoughtfully selected, trained by gifted storytellers, and highly honoured by their peers. In addition, families also transmitted stories through grandparents, aunts and uncles in situations where specific information or lessons were deemed to be needed by young people.

It is not surprising that first translations of legends and myths by well meaning non-Native people were bare story lines and were missing the very essence that made them important to the Native audiences. All the drama of good oral storytelling was often missing, there was no longer any 'Native voice,' and the cultural lessons were often omitted and deemed unnecessary.

Value Themes in Student Stories

In contrast, most of the stories selected for *Courageous Spirits* involve either direct or indirect reference to these highly prized cultural values. In order to provide teachers and students with easy access to the link between stories and values, a categorical listing of eight themes has been compiled with reference to several student stories reflecting examples of these qualities. These themes have been arranged in a series of tables for easy reference.

Students can be encouraged to search for examples of these themes and to share their results. Due to the wholistic nature of 'culture' there will frequently be more than one theme running through the student author's stories. Students may enjoy noting the overlap and interconnectedness.

Bridging to Published Books

Each theme includes a few examples of published Native literature which reinforces a particular value. Teachers may wish to have students select their favourite student stories, analyze the message within, and then select books from the bridging list to read and share with classmates. Authors have been noted as either Native or non-Native so that 'voice' can be compared and contrasted.

The designation **P** for primary level, **I** for intermediate level, and **HS** for high school level is provided for selection of published materials.

All book references are listed in a biography of published materials which begins on page 57.

Values Theme: Respect for Elders/Connections with Past

Courageous Spirits reference	Other published books
My Hero - Trevor Peters (Gr 7) Grandmother - Roberta (Bobbi) White (Gr 8) Letter to Grandfather - Wendy Paul (Gr 10) My Hero, "Dan K. Stevens" Mic Mac - Bradley Stevens (Gr 7)	The Elders Are Watching - Dave Bouchard/Roy Vickers (**P**) Eagle Feather - An Honour - Ferguson Plain (**P**) Annie and the Old One - Miska Miles (**I**) The Whale People - Roderick Haig Brown (**HS**)

Values Theme: Stewardship of Land, Animals, Resources

Courageous Spirits reference	Other published books
My Dad - Jennifer Claxton (Gr 3) An Inuk Hero - Anita Ootoowak (Gr 9) A Life to Know - Samson Ootoowak (Gr 6) Hunting Expedition with My Buddy - Norman Inootik (Gr 8)	Spirit of the White Bison - Beatrice Culleton (**P**) Julie of the Wolves - Jean Craighead George (**I**) How Can One Sell Air? - Chief Seattle (**I**) People of the Deer - Farley Mowatt (**HS**)

Values Theme: Cooperation/Survival

Courageous Spirits reference	Other published books
My Dad - Pat Kotchea (Gr 9) My Father the Chief - Faye Erasmus (Gr 8) Theresa Gadwa: A Native Heroine - Carla Goodrunning (Gr 6) Jean Henry - Mandy Westfall (Gr 5)	Two Little Girls Lost in the Bush - Glecia Bear (**P**) Another World - Pat Bearclaw (**I**) Sweetgrass - Jean Hudson (**HS**)

Values Theme: Spirituality/Health

Courageous Spirits reference	Other published books
Kirsten - Debbie Franki (Gr 10) Aboriginal Hero - Norman Kiguktak (Gr 10) Chief Dan George - Trina Setah (Gr 9) A Friend of the People - Wahsayzee Deleary (Gr 7)	My Home Forever - Laura Boyd (**P**) Return of the Indian Spirit - Phyllis Johnson (**I**) Karnee: A Paiute Narrative - Lella Scott (**HS**)

Values Theme: Hospitality/Generosity	
Courageous Spirits reference	Other published books
My Aboriginal Hero - Dina Williams (Gr 3)	Mountain Goats of Temlahan - William Toye (**P**)
How Eagle Saved Us - Hilary Zornow (Gr 4)	Kwulasulwut - Elder Ellen White (**I**)
Unsung Hero - Mike Wesley (Gr 7)	Stand Tall, My Son - George Clutesi (**HS**)
My Chief - Wilfred Basque (Gr 6)	

Values Theme: Humour, Teasing, Fun	
Courageous Spirits reference	Other published books
My Grandfather - Brandie Cornelius (Gr 6)	I Can't Have Bannock etc. - Bernelda Wheeler (**P**)
Bobby - Alice Bird (Gr 11)	My Name is Seepeetza - Shirley Sterling (**I**)
	Moose Meat and Wild Rice - Basil Johnson (**HS**)

Values Theme: Respect for Differences	
Courageous Spirits reference	Other published books
Where's Home Sweet Home? - Inger-Lise Christensen (Gr 10)	Peter's Moccasins - Nancy McKenzie (**P**)
Aboriginal Hero - Tina Conway (Gr 11)	My Mom is So Unusual - Iris Loewen (**I**)
Jim Compton - Quin Kirkness (Gr 5)	The Broken Cord - Michael Dorris (**HS**)

Values Theme: Personal Responsibility	
Courageous Spirits reference	Other published books
The Way of a Winner - Jesse Bruneau (Gr 8)	Smokehorse - Cliff Faulkner (**P**)
Bill Reid, The Artist - Kiel Russ (Gr 2)	My Name is Louis - Janet Craig James (**I**)
Why I'm Proud to be Aboriginal - Cheyenne Corcoran (Gr 6)	Winners - Mary Ellen Collura (**HS**)
Nelson Bird - Eleanor Shannacappo (Gr 12)	

Additional Reading Choices/Activities for Students

The following activities are described as if directed to the students themselves, so that teachers may copy them and provide them to students at various age levels. Activities have been chosen to match approximate literacy skill levels but will have to be adjusted by knowledge of the particular students.

Primary to Intermediate

1. Read a book or stories from a modern Native author from another culture or province of Canada.

Bernelda Wheeler, Cree, Manitoba
Laura Boyd, Carrier, British Columbia
Ferguson Plain, Ojibway, Ontario
Pat Bearclaw, Ojibway, Ontario
Beatrice Culleton, Manitoba
Simon Paul, Dene, Six Nations, Ontario

2. Prepare a poem or legend to read to a younger child or a group of children.

My Heart Soars, Chief Dan George
The Ballad of Alice Moonchild, Aleota Blythe
Waswanipi, Hugo Muller
Star Quilt, Roberta Whiteman
Song of Eskasoni, More Poems of Rita Joe, Rita Joe
A Modern Anthology of Indian Poetry: Sweetgrass, Orville, Ronald, and W. Keon

3. Read a favourite passage or give a pep talk about a Native author's story or book to a class or a small group.

4. Sample several legends and myths written by both Native and non-Native authors to note the differences.

Paul Goble, Christie Harris, Robert Munsch, William Toye, Anne Simeon, Anne Cameron, Bernelda Wheeler, J.J. Cornplanter, John Joe, Sark, Helen Laboline, Ray Smith, Dean Whitestone, Elder Ellen White, Harry Robinson (Wendy Wickwire), Glecia Bear

5. Read a Native legend from the United States that features coyote or raven to determine if they are similar or different in significant ways.

Intermediate

6. Read trickster stories which show how Raven, Coyote, Wesakejak or Nanabozo use transformation. Find differences or similarities between each character.

Under Coyote's Eye, Henry Biessel
Legends of the Longhouse, J.J. Cornplanter
Nanabush and the Strangler, John McCleod
The Birth of Nanabosho, Joseph McLellan
Tyendinaga Tales, Rona Rustige
Son of Raven, Son of Deer, George Clutesi
Nanna Bijou the Sleeping Giant, Jocelyne Villeneuve
Myths of the Iroquois, E.A. Smith
A Coyote Columbus Story, Thomas King

7. Choose an Elder's story (biography) and read it to an Elder in your family or in your community.

Biographies of Frank Tobuk, John Honea, Joe Beetus, Edwin Simon, Oscar Nictune, Roger Dayton, Henry Beetus of the Yukon, published by Hancock House, in 1980 and 1981. ISBN series 0-88839-064-5 to 0-88839-073-4

8. Prepare poetry favourites and perform with a few classmates from the list under number two.

Intermediate/High School

9. Choose an anthology of Native drama. Select a favourite to read or perform in class.

Write It On Your Heart
The Land Called Morning: Three Plays
Cues and Entrances
Inlook and the Sun

10. Identify a student story or a published story or book that uses three or four interconnecting cultural values in developing the story.

Another World, Pat Bearclaw
The Beet Queen, Louise Erdrich
April Raintree, Beatrice Culleton

11. Read a book that depicts a modern Native hero.

Chief: The Fearless Vision of Billy Diamond, Ron McGregor
To Run with Longboat: 12 Stories of Indian Athletes in Canada,
Brenda Zeman
Assu of Cape Mudge, Harry Assu and Joy Inglis
Stoney Creek Woman, Bridget Moran

High School to Adult

12. Read about modern (current) issues in Native life.

The Broken Cord by Michael Dorris (Fetal Alcohol Syndrome)
Inside Out: An Autobiography by a Native Canadian, James Tyman
(Justice/prison)
Crazywater, Brian Maracle (Alcohol and leadership)
Of Utmost Good Faith, Vine Jr. Deloria (Rights, land claims, property
rights)
Brothers In Arms, Jordan Wheeler (AIDS)
The Book of Jessica, Maria Campbell

13. Select a book or series of readings which describes how survival and historical transmission are dependent on mythology, and the wisdom and guidance of the Native Elders.

Stand Tall, My Son, George Clutesi
The Grieving Indian: An Ojibwe Elder Shares His Discovery of Help
and Hope, H. Arthur with George McPeak
John Tootoosis, Jean Goodwill and Norma Sluman
The Sacred Hoop, Paula Gunn Allen
Rainbow Tribe: Ordinary People Journeying On the Red Road, Ed
McGaa, Eagle Man
Karnee: A Paiute Narrative, Lalla Scott

14. Compare the biographies of a Native Elder and a Native politician from previous references.

Bibliography of Published Materials

Over the past ten years the need for an expanded base of literature and the burgeoning number of Native authors has provided an opportunity for local communities to develop culturally based material. The availability of computer publishing programs has added to this development. As a result there are some excellent sources of material that are not listed in references such as <u>Books In Print</u>.

Wherever these materials are listed as a resource, the local supplier's address and the ISBN number has been included. In a few cases the ISBN numbers were difficult to ascertain. If the usual suppliers have difficulty in ordering any of the books listed below it is suggested that you try ordering through Northwest Coast Book and Art Company, Box 436, 720 Highway 33, Queen Charlotte City, B.C. V0T 1S0, or Theytus Books, 259 Brunswick Street, Penticton, B.C. V2A 5P9.

Please Note: Titles marked with an asterisk are books written by First Nations authors.

* <u>A Coyote Columbus Story</u>. Thomas King. Toronto: Douglas & McIntyre, 1992, ISBN 0-88899-155X.

* <u>Another World</u>. Pat Bearclaw. Scarborough: Self Published temporarily, 1993, no ISBN. Address #7 Muldrew Avenue, Scarborough, Ontario, M1R 1XR.

* <u>A Modern Anthology of Indian Poetry</u>. Orville, Ronald and W. Keon. Elliot Lake: Algoma Printing Services, 1971.

<u>Annie and the Old One</u>. Miska Miles. Toronto: Little Brown & Company, 1971. ISBN 0-316-57120-2.

* <u>Assu of Cape Mudge: Recollections of an Indian Chief</u>. Harry Assu and Joy Inglis. Vancouver: UBC Press, 1989 ISBN 0-7748-0341-X.

<u>The Ballad of Alice Moonchild and Others</u>. Aleota Blythe. Winnipeg: Pemmican Publications, 1981.

* <u>Becoming Brave</u>. Laine Thom. Chronicle Books, 1992, ISBN 0-8818-0163-2.

* The Beet Queen. Louise Erdrich. New York: Bantam, 1989, ISBN 0-553-26807-4.

The Birth of Nanabosho. Joseph McLellan. Winnipeg: Pemmican Publishers, 1989, ISBN 0-921827-00-8.

* Black Elk Speaks. Wallace Black Elk. San Francisco: Harper, 1990, ISBN 0-06-250074-0.

* The Book of Jessica. Maria Campbell and Linda Griffiths. Coach House, 1989, ISBN 0-88910-380-1.

* The Broken Cord. Michael Dorris. New York: Harper Collins, 1989, ISBN 0-06-691682-6.

* Brother In Arms. Jordan Wheeler. Winnipeg: Pemmican Publishers, 1989, ISBN 0-921827-07-5.

Cheryl's Potlatch. Sheila Thompson. Vanderhoof: Yinka Dene Language Institute, 1991, ISBN 1-895267-02-01.

Chief: The Fearless Vision of Billy Diamond. Toronto: Penguin, 1991, ISBN 0-14-012036-X.

* Crazywater. Brian Maracle. Toronto: Penguin/Viking Press, 1993, ISBN 0-670-84659-7.

* The Crying Christmas Tree. Alan Crow. Winnipeg: Pemmican Publishers, 1989, ISBN 0-921827-13-X.

Cues and Entrances. Henry Beissel. Toronto: Playwrights Co-op, 1980.

* Eagle Feather, An Honour. Ferguson Plain. Winnipeg: Pemmican, 1992, ISBN 0-921827-12-1.

* Edwin Simon, A Biography, Huslia. Koyukuk-Yukon School District, North Vancouver: Hancock House, 1981, ISBN 0-88839-068-8.

The Elders are Watching. Dave Bouchard. Tofino, B.C.: Eagle Dancer Enterprises Ltd., 1990, ISBN 0-9693485-3-3.

* <u>Frank Tobuk, A Biography</u>. Evansville, Koyukuk/Yukon Education Department. North Vancouver: Hancock House, 1980, ISBN 0-88839-064-5.

* <u>The Grieving Indian: An Ojibwe Elder Share His Discovery of Help and Hope</u>. H. Arthur with George McPeek. Winnipeg: intertribal Christian Communications Inc., 1988.

* <u>Henry Beetus, A Biography, Hughes</u>. North Vancouver: Hancock House, 1980, ISBN 0-88839-063-7.

* <u>How Can One Sell the Air?</u> Chief Seattle. Northwest Coast Book and Art Company, Box 436, Queen Chaarlotte City, BC, V0T 1S0.

* <u>I Am the Eagle Free (Sky Song)</u>. Simon Paul-Dene. Penticton: Theytus, 1992, ISBN 0-919441-34-3.

* <u>I Can't Have Bannock but the Beaver Has a Dam</u>. Bernalda Wheeler. Winnipeg: Pemmican Publ., 1984, ISBN 0-919143-4-3.

<u>Inlook and the Sun</u>. Henry Beissel. Toronto: Playwrights Co-op. 1980.

* <u>Inside Out: An Autobiography by a Native Canadian</u>. James Tyman. Saskatoon: Fifth House, 1990, ISBN 0-920079-58.

* <u>Joe Beetus, A Biography, Hughes</u>. Koyukuk/Yukon Education Department. North Vancouver: Hancock House, 1980, ISBN 0-88839-065-3.

* <u>John Honea, A Biography, Ruby</u>. Koyukuk/Yukon Education Department. North Vancouver: Hancock House, 1981, ISBN 0-88839-073-4.

* <u>John Tootoosis</u>. Jean Goodwill and Norma Sluman. Winnipeg: Pemmican Publishers, 1984, ISBN 0-919143-39-3.

<u>Julie of the Wolves</u>. Jean Craighead George. New York: Harper and Row, 1972, ISBN 0-06-440058.

<u>Karnee: A Paiute Narrative</u>. Lalla Scott. Reno: University of Nevada Press, 1984, ISBN 0-87417-189-X.

* <u>Kwulasulwut</u>. Elder Ellen White. Penticton: Theytus, 1992, ISBN 0-919441-04-1.

<u>Land Called Morning: Three Plays</u>. Caroline Heath, ed. Fifth House, 1986, ISBN 0-920079-24-5.

* <u>Legends of the Longhouse</u>. Jesse Cornplanter. Iroqrafts, 1986, ISBN 0-9919645-13-5.

* <u>Moose Meat and Wild Rice</u>. Basil Johnson. Toronto: McLelland-Stewart, 1988, ISBN 0-7710-4444-5.

<u>Mountain Goats of Temlahan</u>. William Toye. Toronto: Oxford Press, 1988, ISBN 0-19-540278-2.

* <u>My Heart Soars</u>. Chief Dan George. North Vancouver: Hancock House, 1981, ISBN 0-88839-231-1.

* <u>My Home Forever</u>. Laura Boyd. Quesnel: Developing Our Resources Curriculum, Apple McIntosh Desktop Publishing, 1990, ISBN 0-9693638-07.

<u>My Mom is So Unusual</u>. Iris Loewen. Winnipeg: Pemmican Publishers, 1986, ISBN 0-919143-37-7.

<u>My Name is Louis</u>. Janet Craig James. Waterloo, Ont.: Penumbra, 1988, ISBN 0-921254-06-7.

<u>My Name is Seepeetza</u>. Shirley Sterling. Toronto: Douglas and McIntyre, 1992, ISBN 0-88899-165-7.

<u>Myths of the Iroquois</u>. E.A. Smith. Washington, D.C.: US Bureau of American Ethnology, 1983.

<u>Nanabosho Steals Fire</u>. Joseph McLellan. Winnipeg: Pemmican, 1990, ISBN 0-921827-05-9.

<u>Nanabush and the Stranger: An Ojibway Tale on Diabetes</u>. John McLeod. Toronto: University Press, 1981.

<u>Nanna Bijou, the Sleeping Giant</u>. Jocelyne Villeneuve. Moonbeam, Ontario: Penumbra Press, 1981, ISBN 0-920-806-26-0.

* <u>Of Utmost Good Faith</u>. Vine Deloria. New York: Bantam, 1971.

* <u>Oscar Nictune, A Biography, Alatna</u>. Kuyukuk/Yukon Education Department. North Vancouver: Hancock House, 1980, ISBN 0-88839-062-9.

<u>People of the Deer</u>. Farley Mowat. Seal Publ., 1980, ISBN 0-7704-2254-3.

<u>Peter's Moccasins</u>. Dan Truss and Nancy MacKenzie, eds. Edmonton: Reidmore, 1987, ISBN 0-919091-24-5.

* <u>Rainbow Tribe</u>. Ed McGaa, Eagle Man. San Francisco: Harper, 1992, ISBN 0-06-250661-0.

<u>Return of the Indian Spirit</u>. Vinson Brown. Berkeley: Celestial Arts, 1981, ISBN 0-89807-401-8.

* <u>Roger Dayton, A Biography, Koyukuk</u>. Koyukuk/Yukon Education Department. North Vancouver: Hancock House, 1981, ISBN 0-88839-067-X.

* <u>The Sacred Hoop</u>. Paula Gunn Allen. Boston: Beacon Press, 1986.

<u>Smoke Horse</u>. Cliff Faulkner. Toronto: McLelland & Stewart, 1968.

* <u>Son of Raven, Son of Deer: Fables of the Tse-Shaht People</u>. George Clutesi. Sidney: Grays Publishing, 1967.

* <u>Song of Eskasoni, More Poems of Rita Joe</u>. Rita Joe. Charlottetown, PEI: Ragweed Press, 1988, ISBN 0-920304-85-0.

* <u>Spirit of the White Bison</u>. Beatrice Culleton. Winnipeg: Pemmican Publishers, 1988, ISBN 0-919143-40-7.

* <u>Stand Tall, My Son</u>. George Clutesi. Victoria: Newport Bay Publishers, 1990, ISBN 0-921513-03-8.

* <u>Star Quilt</u>. Roberta Hill Whiteman. Minneapolis, Minn: Holy Cow! Press, 1984.

<u>Stoney Creek Woman</u>. Bridget Moran. Vancouver: Arsenal Pulp Press, 1990, ISBN 0-88978-197-4.

<u>To Run with Longboat: Twelve Stories</u>. Brenda Zeman. GMS Ventures, 1988, ISBN 0-9692320-1-2.

Two Little Girls Lost in the Bush. Glecia Bear (F. Ahenakew). Saskatoon: Fifth House Publishers, 1991, ISBN 0-920079-77-6.

* Two Pair of Shoes. Esther Sanderson. Winnipeg: Pemmican Publishers, 1992, ISBN 0-921827-15-6.

Tyendinaga Tales. Rona Rustige. Montreal: McGill University Queens Press, 1988, ISBN 0-7735-0650-0.

Under Coyote's Eye. Henry Beissel. Alexandria, Ontario: Arlette Franciere, 1978.

Waswanipi. Hugo Muller. Toronto: Anglican Book Centre, 1976.

The Whale People. Roderick Haig-Brown. Toronto: Collins, 1986, ISBN 0-00-222197-7.

Write It On Your Heart. Harry Robinson & Wendy Wickwire. Vancouver: Talon Books, 1989, ISBN 0-888922-273-8.

THEME UNIT:

WRITING PROJECT ON ABORIGINAL HEROES

(ADAPTED FROM ORIGINAL CONTEST GUIDELINES FOR TEACHERS)

INTRODUCTION

As has been stated, Courageous Spirits *had its origins in a national writing contest for Aboriginal students. Included in the contest information package were some guidelines for teachers, including suggestions for varying the scope of the teaching unit; a concepts and definitions section for introducing the contest; culturally sensitive research approaches; a sequential approach to the writing; and some additional considerations to guide student writing.*

Those guidelines are reproduced here in a slightly modified form for teachers to use as a 4 - 6 week theme unit for students to write about their Aboriginal heroes .

The writing process is a difficult one for nearly everyone, and it is not our pretense here to lay out a blueprint for successful teaching of writing. We can say, however, that in our minds the role of the teacher in providing a supportive, open, question-raising, accepting environment in which children can feel safe to explore ideas is a keystone to the encouragement of creativity in the classroom.

Because these guidelines cover teaching from kindergarten through grade 12, we begin with the assumption that teachers will adapt those ideas they care to use to the level of their students. We also trust that where our suggestions fail to take into account the particulars of their situation, they will take a forgiving attitude.

ORGANIZATION OF UNIT

This unit is divided into four sections (1) a teaching overview, (2) concepts and definitions, (3) putting the concepts into action,

including a sample sequential approach, and (4) two additional teaching considerations.

SECTION ONE: A TEACHING OVERVIEW

1.) Scope

Some schools may decide to enter wholeheartedly into a writing project as a means of involving the whole community in a *theme unit of research and writing about Aboriginal Heroes.* If so, innovative teachers will find many possibilities for integrating subject areas—social studies (to examine geographic areas that are the home cultural regions of heroes identified by the students); science (to consider environmental heroes); music (contemporary songs sung by well-known Aboriginal singers); and many ideas to relate language arts, art, careers, history, and cultural studies to the project. Interviewing local Elders, politicians, entrepreneurs, artists, police, firefighters, loggers, fishermen—nearly anyone—can be a productive way for students to learn of acts of heroism and the people behind those actions. Library displays, newsletters, bulletin boards, radio skits, poster contests and many other activities can support the theme. Some fairly ambitious projects requiring considerable organization might be sparked by the theme unit.

At the other end of the scale, one individual teacher may encourage his or her lone Aboriginal student to use the theme of Aboriginal Heroes as a device for motivating writing, and see what develops.

In between the extremes, classroom teachers may decide the Aboriginal Heroes theme is just what they've been looking for to do some workshop writing with their students for a four to six week unit. If so, some preparatory work may be needed, including:

- Planning and preparation for teaching (may include collaborative planning amongst teachers, particularly for integration of subjects)

- Gaining support and cooperation from community members

- Collaborative planning (school staff, community people: consider cultural sensitivity and appropriateness of research process, contest parameters, judging process, celebrating all participant efforts).

Whatever the case, planning will be fundamental to the implementation of most writing projects, and it is our hope that what follows will be of assistance to teachers who are always pressed for planning time.

2.) Sequence

A helpful view for preparing to implement this writing project is to plan for three major components in the following sequence:

Readiness stage

Research stage

Writing stage

The remaining sections of this guide offer suggestions for these three stages with specific reference to the theme: researching and writing about Aboriginal Heroes.

SECTION TWO: CONCEPTS AND DEFINITIONS

A useful place to begin the Aboriginal Heroes project at any grade level is to **clarify key concepts and definitions** in order to develop understandings helpful to the research and writing phases of the project. This could be called the Readiness Stage of the project.

Sensitivity to the cultural context is of primary importance, and this respectful approach can set the tone for the entire project. A hero in one cultural context may be a bully in another—so definitions should reflect cultural values. Respectful, non-judgmental questioning techniques prove of immense importance here. The teacher's best role is that of a facilitator to create an atmosphere where students can freely express their *own* definitions and values about their heroes.

The three concepts/definitions groups that follow could be taught in three or more lessons as will be outlined shortly.

      A. Concept/definition Group One:
            Aboriginal, First Nations, Native, Indian, Metis, Inuit, local tribal/clan name

      B. Concept/definition Group Two:
            Hero, heroine, unsung hero, famous hero

      C. Concept/definition Three:
            Research

Developing common understandings at the beginning of the unit will provide a more secure framework for the writing project.

The teacher's judgment is most important here. Some students will have very clear concepts already; others, especially in the lower grades, will need more time and several activities to reach a level of readiness sufficient to undertake the research and writing that the project asks of them.

A: CONCEPT/DEFINITION GROUP ONE: ONE LESSON

Aboriginal, First Nations, Native, Indian, Metis, Inuit, local tribal/clan name

Most older Aboriginal students will have some familiarity with most or all of these terms, but may not have a sense of connectivity with the concept of "Aboriginal peoples." That's okay. The intention of this activity is to develop realizations that there are many ways that Aboriginal people across Canada describe themselves—Dene, Haida, Micmac—but that other terms like "Aboriginal," "First Nations," "Metis," and "Inuit" are used to show *a common affiliation* among many different Aboriginal groups. The labels aren't important—the feeling of belonging is.

The intention is **not** to make distinctions which separate and label people, or to examine the legal ramifications of definitions and distinctions. Far from it. Rather, a positive sense of belonging should be encouraged—a sense of identity with a group; the commonalities. These are concepts that can be encouraged as writing themes, especially since heroes often bring into focus the values which unify groups of people, and define for us who we are. Take time to underscore some of these promising themes as they arise to help start those creative motors. (*There's* a good idea for a play/story/poem. What do you suppose you could do with *that* idea?)

With all age groups, teachers could begin with a review of the local Aboriginal name (or names) that students identify with. Ask students for other names used for other Aboriginal peoples—in other regions, the province or territory, and across Canada—that they know of. (Extension activities: Begin a newspaper article collection about Aboriginal peoples. Maps of Aboriginal groups could be displayed. Have someone from the community come in to share some cultural history.)

Some discussion could take place on why this common naming or grouping occurs; use the comparison of why people identify themselves as British Columbians or Canadians or North Americans.

Keep this lesson short—don't belabour it. These are not easy concepts, and the children need time to think about these ideas. But by posing some hard questions you are creating readiness, sending the message that you respect the children's ability to think, and laying the groundwork for the next step in the writing process. (First

the questions, then the thinking, then the discussing and researching, then the lists of ideas, arrangement of ideas, sentence formation, writing, and re-writing, and re-writing and so on.)

End this discussion, perhaps, by asking students to think of some famous Aboriginal people they know for discussion during next class. This will serve as a transition to the second concept/definition group.

B: CONCEPT/DEFINITION GROUP TWO: ONE OR MORE LESSONS

Hero, heroine, unsung hero, famous hero

Teachers may want to use stories, contemporary songs, movies or videos about a hero of their own, or about an Aboriginal hero to introduce the concept of "heroes."

At some grade levels, having students use dictionaries to find out what the definitions are for "hero" and "heroine" may be useful. (For the purposes of this project we have used the term "hero" to include both women and men.) The qualities of character, action or behaviour, and the motivational and inspirational influence upon others are what we consider important in determining who a "hero" is. Aboriginal cultures may have different traditional ways of identifying and relating to the concept of "hero." The advice and assistance of the local Aboriginal community is recommended.

The negative side of hero worship could also be a productive topic for discussion, particularly for older students.

Students could discuss the qualities that, in their view, make a hero, then make a list of their heroes (not limited to Aboriginal heroes). Their heroes could be real people, past or present, or fictional characters from cartoons, comics, literature, TV, movies. The following questions may help stimulate thought: (small group discussion?? 2 questions each?? 5 minute limit?? someone *record* notes??)

- What *makes* someone a hero to you?
- What have some people *done* (action) to become a hero?
- What *qualities* do we *admire* in a hero?
- What *influence* or *effect* does the hero have on us?
- How do we *honour* heroes? Why?
- Why is it important for us to *have* heroes?

Discuss the concept of "unsung" heroes. Then go back to the students' list asking them to distinguish between "famous" and "unsung" heroes, and to add students' suggestions about unknown

people who have committed worthy acts of courage, etc.—preferably people from their own community.

If it is needed, move the focus to Aboriginal heroes. If the listing of Aboriginal heroes is not as extensive as the general list, it should be noted, and some thoughts shared on why this is so. (The need for projects such as this Aboriginal Heroes book project could be mentioned.)

Ways of exploring the *cultural* concept and meaning of "heroes" may include:

- examining the Aboriginal language for the way someone who is like a hero is described, a similar term for hero.
- why and how the local community honour people for their achievements, what is used to symbolize honour and respect (for example, the eagle feather).
- who would be heroes from the local community and why?
- are there any historic people, or characters from stories or dance that could be considered heroes?

Be guided by your students level of participation and interest as to the amount of time you spend on this topic. Let them know that they will be researching a hero of their own to write about. Who might that be?

C: CONCEPT/DEFINITION GROUP THREE: ONE OR MORE LESSONS

Research

Some questions which could stimulate class discussion on the topic of research follow, but will need to be modified according to the grade level of the students. Sensitivity to the cultural context is important to establishing appropriate research approaches (questioning techniques, phrasing of the questions, being careful not to violate cultural practices). This suggests a role for community participants to clarify appropriate practices.

- What do you think "research" is? (Dictionaries may be used to check against students' ideas.)
- What kinds of research have you heard about?
- Why do people do research?
- Who does research? (The scope of answers could range from scientists, to university academics, to work done in the local cultural centre or land claims office, to the teachers' and students' preparation for writing reports, etc.)
- How is research done by those particular groups? (How do research methods differ?)
- What is the importance of research?

- What are some problems or issues that are created because of research? (i.e., objection to testing on animals, how people are treated, who owns the research information, misuse of research information, methods are not appropriate)

Remember that this is a *readiness* exercise, and should lead to the major question for each student's consideration: What role will research play in preparing my story? Emphasize the 5W-H here: (who, what, why, where, when and how) to assist students in framing their own research questions. Try a dry run to help students follow the sequence of steps, ideas, and activities underlying the research component of their writing.

Extension Activities:
1. Collect news articles about research related issues. Have students note the way research was done and what impact it can have on people, animals, and environment. What problems were identified?
2. Invite people who do research to the school as guest speakers to talk about how they do research, why their work is important, and what some of the problems are.
3. Visit local services in the community that do research such as a cultural centre or land claims office. Students can develop specific questions that they could ask or find answers to during their visit.
4. Cultural speakers may be invited to the school to talk about how they traditionally used methods of careful "inquiry" to learn or to investigate a problem. They could also talk about how one could show respect (cultural protocol) to Elders and others who the students may speak to or interview. For example, students should know if it is culturally correct and proper to bring a gift or offering to the person they will interview. They should know what would be considered rude or disrespectful behaviour. Aboriginal language words/phrases may be taught to the students that are related to research inquiry.

SECTION THREE: PUTTING THE CONCEPTS INTO ACTION: A SAMPLE SEQUENTIAL APPROACH

Once the class has discussed and shown an understanding of the three concepts/definitions groups (*Aboriginal, hero and research*), they could share their ideas of who they would pick as a hero to

research and write about. (To pose the research question: Who would I choose as an Aboriginal hero and why?)

The following is a sequential list of ideas that teachers might modify to suit their grade level. It is offered to help students organize their approach to the writing project using *research methodology consistent with cultural ways*. It is also a 5W-H approach:

a.) first, choose a hero to research (*who* could I choose as an Aboriginal hero to write about?)

b.) choose a research method (*how* will I go about getting information?)

c.) collect the information (*who* can I interview, *where* can I find written information, *where* is Haida Gwaii?)

d.) examine the data collected for useful ideas (*what* details could I use to describe actions, for dialogue in my play, to give impact to my story, to help my readers understand why this person is important?)

e.) organize the ideas in preparation for writing (an outline—*what* comes first, second...)

f.) choose a writing form (poem, play, story, essay)

g.) write the first draft

h.) get feedback from peers, teacher, parent, sibling (*how* can I improve my work? *what* is best about my story?) If students have interviewed people, they should show them what they have written and ask for their approval of the written work (ethical considerations)

i.) revise for style, clarity, impact

j.) final revision for mechanics and appearance (and for submission to school paper, etc.) Students as a group could decide what kind of standards should be considered for the final draft. Students might also consider collecting all final drafts into a class/school newspaper for the benefit of the whole school community.

SECTION FOUR: SOME ADDITIONAL TEACHING CONSIDERATIONS

The preceding sections have dealt with issues of cultural sensitivity, the teacher's role as facilitator of student-based definitions and concepts, and approaches to integrating subject matter. There remain two additional considerations that occur to us:

The Use of Imagination
Besides learning factual information, students should be encouraged to use their imaginations to relate to the heroes in an affective,

empathic manner. Questions that could help
students do this include:

   a.) Why would I want to be like this hero?
       (What qualities do I admire about this hero? Are there
       some weaknesses as well?)
   b.) Why does the world need more people like this hero?
   c.) How has this hero affected me? (feelings, aspirations)
   d.) How has this hero influenced how I or others feel about my
       culture?
   e.) What kind of dialogue could arise from the heroes actions?
   f.) What dramatic moments can I see in my mind's eye?
   g.) What sounds, sights, smells, textures, can I hear, see,
       smell, feel?

Challenging Thinking and Inspiring Creative Thought
The very concept of heroes captures in its own way some of the
spirit behind this writing project—to consider those who have
exceeded the normal bounds that seem to limit human endeavour,
and to be able to recognize the gifts that lie within all of us. We want
to celebrate the fact that as Aboriginal people we have survived
generations of assault to our self-esteem and to our cultural ways.
Who helped us survive, and how? What values lay at the heart of
their actions, and what is their lesson to the world? How might all
Canadians be enriched by their example?

Through this project, we would like to communicate to students that
everyone has something of the heroic in her or him; that everyone
can think deeply and feel deeply about issues of importance; and
that everyone can learn to express those feelings and thoughts in
written words.

RELATED READING

The following books are recommended as sources of information about some of the topics raised in this guide.

Allen, P. (1989). <u>Spider woman's granddaughters</u>. Boston: Beacon Press.

Bopp, J., Bopp, M., Brown, L., & Lane, P. (1984). <u>The sacred tree</u>. Lethbridge, Alberta: Four Worlds Development Press, University of Lethbridge.

Caduto, M.J., & Bruchac, J. (1988). <u>Keepers of the earth: Teachers guide</u>. Saskatoon, Saskatchewan: Fifth House Publishers.

Caduto, M.J., & Bruchac, J. (1989). <u>Keepers of the earth: Native stories and environmental activities for children</u>. Saskatoon, Saskatchewan: Fifth House Publishers.

Caduto, M.J., & Bruchac, J. (1991). <u>The native stories from Keepers of the earth: Told by Joseph Bruchac</u>. Saskatoon, Saskatchewan: Fifth House Publishers.

Egan, K. (1992). <u>Imagination in teaching and learning: The middle school years</u>. London, Ontario: The Althouse Press, The University of Western Ontario.

Egan, K. (1986). <u>Teaching as story telling</u>. London, Ontario: The Althouse Press, The University of Western Ontario.

Friesen, V., Archibald, J., & Jack, R. (1992). <u>Creating cultural awareness about First Nations: A workshop guide</u>. Available from the Ministry of Education, Aboriginal Education Branch, Parliament Bldgs., Victoria, BC.

Gazda, G. M., et al. (1984). <u>Human relations development: A manual for educators</u> (3rd ed.). Toronto: Allyn and Bacon, Inc.

George, Chief Dan, & Hirnschall, H. (1974/1989). <u>My heart soars</u>. Surrey, BC: Hancock House.

Johnson, D. W., Johnson, R. T., Holubec, E. J., & Roy, P. (1984). <u>Circles of learning</u>. ISBN: 0-87120-123-2.

Keeshig-Tobias, L. (1990, January 26). Stop stealing Native stories. <u>The Globe and Mail</u>.

King, T. (1990). <u>All my relations</u>. Toronto: McClelland & Stewart.

Lightning, W. (1992). Compassionate mind: Implications of a text written by Elder Louis Sunchild. <u>Canadian Journal of Native education</u>, <u>19</u>(2), 215-253, [cites Wapaskwan (1991). Untitled, unpublished manuscript concerning metaphor in First Nations stories].

Marashio, P. (1982). Enlighten my mind. <u>Journal of American Indian Education</u>, <u>22</u>(2), 2-10.

McLain, G. (1990). <u>The Indian way: Learning to communicate with mother earth</u>. Santa Fe, New Mexico: John Muir Publications.

McLuhan, T. C. (1971). <u>Touch the earth: A self-portrait of Indian existence</u>. New York: Promontory Press.

Miller, J. P. (1988). <u>The holistic curriculum</u>. Toronto: OISE Press.

Miller, J. P., Cassie, J. R. B., & Drake, S. M. (1990). <u>Holistic learning: A teacher's guide to integrated studies</u>. Toronto: OISE Press.

Mokakit Education Research Association. (1992). <u>First Nations freedom: A curriculum of choice (Alcohol, drug and substance abuse prevention) Kindergarten to grade 8</u>.[For information: 59 Sage Crescent, Winnipeg, Manitoba R2Y 0X8]

National Indian Brotherhood. (1972). <u>Indian control of Indian education</u>.

Neihardt, J. G. (1961). <u>Black Elk speaks</u>. Lincoln, Nebraska: University of Nebraska Press.

Silko, L. (1981). <u>Storyteller</u>. New York: Seaver Books.

Ywahoo, D. (1987). <u>Voices of our ancestors: Cherokee teachings from the wisdom fire</u>. Boston: Shambhala.

**This document was prepared for
Mokakit Education Research Association
Faculty of Education, UBC
Vancouver, BC V6T 1Z4**

MOKAKIT is a Blackfoot word which means *to strive for wisdom*.

A Note About the Authors

This Guide was written, designed, and edited by Jo-ann Archibald and Val Friesen.

Jo-ann Archibald, M.Ed., is from the Sto:lo Nation, in B.C.'s Fraser Valley. She is the President of Mokakit Education Research Association and works at the First Nations House of Learning at the University of British Columbia. She has taught in B.C. public schools and at the University of British Columbia, where she was Supervisor of the Native Indian Teacher Education Program (NITEP). Jo-ann is also advisor to the T''skel graduate program at UBC, and is presently completing her doctorate at Simon Fraser University.

Val Friesen, M.A. (Educ), is an education consultant in Vancouver. He has worked extensively in First Nations education development, teacher education, curriculum development, program evaluation, and as a consultant to numerous innovative First Nations initiatives. In addition to co-writing and co-editing this Guide, Val did the typesetting and layout.

Peg Klesner, M.A., who contributed the section Beyond *Courageous Spirits...*, *i*s a reading specialist who worked extensively with First Nations students before her recent retirement from teaching.